30 Minute Vegetarian

30 Minute Vegetarian Mexican Cookbook

Sarah Beattie

Thorsons
An Imprint of HarperCollins*Publishers*

Thorsons
An Imprint of HarperCollins*Publishers*
77–85 Fulham Palace Road,
Hammersmith, London W6 8JB

Published by Thorsons 1997
1 3 5 7 9 10 8 6 4 2

A catalogue record for this book
is available from the British Library

ISBN 0 7225 3426 4

Printed and bound in Great Britain by
Caledonian International Book Manufacturing Ltd, Glasgow

Contents

Thanks are due to: Donna Sclater; Sue Sharpe; Roz Denny, Tony at Sky Co, Tom at Rio Pacific and Dougie Bell's Lupe Pinto on the Great Nopalito Hunt; Pickering Library; *Lonely Planet* & *Rough Guide* to Mexico; Rick and Deann Bayless' *Authentic Mexican Cooking* – an invaluable reference book; Alan Balfour for Apple juice; Wendy Coslett who is not responsible for any errors in my Spanish; Wanda Whiteley and most particularly to Clarissa Hyman.

Love and grateful thanks to Magdalena Gray, Dylan Beattie and especially Michael Gray for services above and beyond.

Introduction

Mexican food has long been popular in the USA, especially in Texas and the South West. It is now finding fans across the rest of the world.

Some of the traditional recipes took hours, if not days, to prepare. In this book shortcuts using modern kitchen slaves (the food processor, mixer and blender) have been found whilst avoiding the sacrifice of flavour. Influences from all over Mexico's diverse regions and from TexMex and CalMex have shaped the recipes.

The ancient Maya people called themselves the Children of the Corn. In many ways present day Mexicans continue to be children of the corn. Corn is in tortillas, tamales, as vegetables, in soups, stews, drinks and puddings. But Mexicans are skilled at making this basic foodstuff interesting. From crisp and crunchy to soft and light, cornmeal is deliciously versatile.

Chillies in dried and fresh guises wake up the flavours of Mexico: some are brightly fiery, some are sweetly mellow. Sharper notes are brought in with limes and tomatillos (little green tomatoes). The unctuousness of smooth avocados and thick soured cream tempers the heat. Flavoursome tomatoes add body to sauces. Beans are the backbone of many meals with fresh cheeses and herbs to supplement them. Chocolate, once the food of the gods in Ancient Mexico, is found in rich savoury sauces and warming drinks, spices lifting them far beyond childhood's hot cocoa.

Mexican food is just right in the depths of a dreary winter but is equally at home in the garden on a balmy summer evening. It is great party food, picnic fare and for barbecues. The main ingredients are cheap, the preparation is often simple and makes wholesome, filling family meals.

Stocking Up – Mexican Ingredients

If you are going to cook Mexican food there are some ingredients you will have to find. What follows is a simple list with some suggested alternatives, in case items are unavailable. British readers will have the most difficulty in tracking down the few obscure items, therefore specialist mail order suppliers are included where appropriate.

Avocados

Mexicans eat more avocados per head of population than any other nation. Buy under-ripe and allow them to ripen in the fruit bowl. Avoid chilling as this deadens the flavour. Mexican Hass ones are available in Europe and are more appropriate than the Israeli Nabal and Fuerte varieties. An avocado is ready when the flesh gives under gentle pressure. In the Hass variety the skin turns from green to black.

Cheese

Mexican cheeses, particularly the fresh ones, are rarely found in Britain although in the USA they are available in some outlets. Appropriate substitutions have therefore been made throughout the book.

Chillies

It would be possible to write a book just on Mexican chillies – there are hundreds of different chillies, they are available fresh, tinned or dried and they can have different names depending on the state they are in. But don't panic – here is a short guide. It is by no means comprehensive but will suffice as an introduction. When you have become addicted to the chillies you can find out more.

FRESH

Habanero – this is a squat, bright yellowy orange chilli when ripe, very hot. Similar to the Jamaican Scotch Bonnet which can be used instead.

Jalapeño – moderate to hot bullet shaped, usually green but sometimes red.

Poblano – a snub-nosed, large green chilli, only moderately hot with a rich flavour. If unavailable use Kenyan or Anaheim.

Serrano – small, thin mostly green. Quite hot. Use small plain green chillies if unavailable.

DRIED

Ancho – this is a dried Poblano, all wrinkly and dark reddy brown. Not very hot and quite fruity.

Chipotle – smoked Jalapeños, with a fiery earthy flavour.

Guajillo – moderate, with an almost apricot tang – some describe it as 'green tea' flavour.

Mulato – apart from being darker, this chilli looks very similar to the Ancho. It is full-flavoured, a little smoky and moderately hot.

New Mexico Red – large mild chilli, fairly sweet.

Pasado – a roasted dried chilli with fruity flavours.

Pasilla – sometimes sold as Negro due to its blackish skin. Moderately hot with a taste of Pomfret cakes and raisins. A slightly smoky scent.

Note

Several of these dried chillies are available in powdered form – this can save considerable cooking time and it is a useful way of adding extra flavour quickly. Many of these dried chillies are not sold by British supermarkets. Check out specialist mail order companies and delicatessens. Recommended are The Cool Chile Company, PO Box 5702, London W11 2GS (mail order only) and Lupe Pinto, 24 Leven Street, Edinburgh (personal callers only). If you have a Mexican restaurant nearby ask them who their suppliers are.

CANNED

Chipotle – the smoked Jalapeño is available canned.
Green – unnamed green chillies are available, peeled and canned.
Serrano – available pickled.

Chocolate

Ibarra Mexican cooking chocolate can be found through specialist shops. It contains sugar, cinnamon and almonds. Green & Black's Maya Gold is quite widely available in the UK. If you cannot find it, use a good plain chocolate with some cinnamon as directed in the recipes.

Corn

Corn is the most commonly used cereal in Mexican cooking. For speed, instant polenta (Italian part-cooked cornmeal) is used in some recipes. If this is not specified then regular, medium ground cornmeal (maize meal) is to be used. Do not confuse with 'cornflour' (cornstarch) – the fine white thickening agent. Sweetcorn (on the cob) is also eaten but to save time canned or frozen kernels are substituted. Ready-made corn tortillas are available in various forms – the best come in sealed cans interleaved with greaseproof paper. Try the various sorts and find a brand you like. If you are going to make your own regularly, you will need to invest in a tortilla press – see good kitchen equipment specialists and department stores. Corn tortillas are made with *masa harina* – a treated corn meal, it has been limed (lime is added to increase the nutritional value of the corn meal), soaked, ground with water and then dried and powdered.

Flour Tortillas

Long life wheat flour tortillas are sold in many supermarkets. It is well worth keeping a couple of packets in the larder for quick meals.

Herbs

Mexicans use *epazote*, also known as pigweed or wormseed. I have been unable to find it in Britain so have not included it in any of the recipes in this book. It has a rather rank, bitter pungent flavour. I suspect that it is used mainly for its medicinal properties – it is a vermifuge, ridding the body of intestinal worms! Other herbs are used as flavoursome alternatives. Coriander (cilantro) is also widely used in Mexican cooking and it is well worth cultivating even if you only have room for a pot on the windowsill. Marjoram or oregano and parsley are also used.

Nopales or Nopalitos

These are cactus stems. Although they are available fresh in the USA, they can only be found bottled or canned in Britain – and then only in specialised outlets (see Lupe Pinto, under Chillies). To use fresh cactus requires very time consuming preparation which would put it out of the scope of this book. Commercially prepared cactus salsa is available.

Oil

Except where otherwise specified, use a good corn or vegetable oil.

Rice

Carolina or Java rice – the shorter of the long grains are the closest to Mexican rice that are widely available.

Soured Cream

Mexican soured cream is thicker than the dairy product available in the UK and USA – use crème fraîche or smetana for a more authentic texture and flavour.

Sugar

Traditional Mexican cooks use an unrefined sugar that comes in hard cones – much like the palm sugar or jaggery of South East Asia. As this is not readily available, light muscovado sugar has been substituted.

Tomatillos

Small green 'tomatoes' in papery husks like physalis (Cape Gooseberries). Available fresh in the USA and very limited outlets in the UK. You are more likely to be able to find them canned. They are not the same as under ripe tomatoes *but* if you have some unripe cherry tomatoes you can use them, provided you salt them first to draw out any bitterness. If the tomatillos are added to a sauce for piquancy, substitute chopped gherkins or capers for a similar flavour.

Tomatoes

Flavoursome tomatoes, especially the plum and Marmande varieties should be used when fresh are called for. Canned tomatoes and passata (strained tomatoes) are often used for speed.

Basic Recipes

Corn Tortillas

Corn tortillas are more widely used in Mexico, the wheat flour ones are normally only found in the north. However, they are much more difficult to make at home as you require *masa harina*, a cornmeal flour that has been specially prepared by soaking it in lime water; and to make life a little easier, a tortilla press. Canned, uncooked tortillas are available as are pre-cooked ones that require reheating. If however you fancy a spot of DIY, here is the recipe. Two people will make much faster work of this, build up a rhythm – one to press and one to cook – and it can be done in 20 minutes.

MAKES 12 TORTILLAS

250 g/9 oz/1½ cups	*masa harina*
250 ml/9 fl oz/1 cup	warm water
a good pinch	of salt
24 squares	of baking paper approx. 20cm / 8in

1) Place all the ingredients in a food processor with the kneading attachment and process for 3–5 minutes.
2) Cover the base of the tortilla press with a square of baking parchment.
3) Pinch off a piece of dough the size of a walnut, put it on the paper. Cover with a second sheet of paper and close the press.
4) Open and peel off the top sheet of paper. If it sticks, the dough is too wet, return to the processor with a little more *masa harina*. If the edges are cracked and crumbly the dough is too dry, return to the processor with 1 teaspoon of water. If it comes away from the paper and the edges are smooth, form the rest of the tortillas in the same way between two sheets of paper.
5) Invert a tortilla onto a moderately hot griddle or heavy frying pan. Peel off the paper backing. Cook for 1–2 minutes either side, until lightly speckledly brown.
6) Remove and place on a clean tea towel where it will soften as it cools. For crisp tortillas or tacos, fry before serving.

Flour Tortillas

Flour tortillas are available ready made in most supermarkets. They have a shelf life of several months or they can be frozen. It is always worth keeping a few packets in your store cupboard.

It isn't very time consuming to make your own though and it is very satisfying. Using a food processor means there's no donkey work and you can double the quantities to stock the freezer with home-made tortillas.

MAKES 16–24 TORTILLAS

500 g/1 lb 2 oz/4½ cups	plain flour
1–2 x 5 ml spoons/	
1–2 teaspoons	salt
75 g/3 oz	white vegetable fat or margarine,
	cut into small pieces
	boiling water

1) Place the flour and salt in the food processor with the kneading attachment and mix.
2) Put the fat into a heatproof measuring jug. Pour on the boiling water up to the 250 ml/9 fl oz/1 cup mark. Stir to melt the fat.
3) Pour into the food processor on a low speed. Continue processing for 3 minutes, as the dough forms into a soft ball.
4) Divide into 24 or 16 pieces or just pinch off walnut-sized pieces of dough as you need them. Keep the rest of the dough covered (the processor bowl with the lid on is ideal). Roll out the balls of dough very thinly.
5) Place on a moderately hot ungreased griddle or heavy frying pan (skillet). Cook for 1 minute on the first side and 30 seconds on the other.
6) Pile onto foil or baking paper as they cook, then reheat loosely wrapped for 2–3 minutes in a moderate oven.
7) You can freeze interleaved with baking paper and wrapped or in a plastic box. To cook from frozen, place on the griddle for 30 seconds each side.

Quick Tamales

Tamal purists will probably throw up their hands in horror – tamal making is normally such a long winded affair. However, these tasty torpedoes of cornmeal flecked with chilli are tender from steaming, are really good with just-melted butter and can be made in under 30 minutes.

Strictly speaking, tamales are steamed, wrapped in corn husks or banana leaves. As these two items are not easily available, have ready 12 squares of baking paper.

Other salsa or moles can be used to accompany them. A Sweet Tamales recipe is to be found on page 131.

SERVES 4–6

285 ml/10 fl oz/1⅓ cups	vegetable stock or water
175 g/6 oz/1 cup	instant polenta
1–2 x 5 ml spoons/ 1–2 teaspoons	coarsely ground red chilli
2.5 ml spoons/½ teaspoon	salt
30 g/1 oz/1 tablespoon	butter or margarine
2 x 5 ml spoons/2 teaspoons	baking powder

1) Mix all the ingredients together in a saucepan and cook over a moderate heat until the mixture is thick and leaves the sides of the pan. Beat well.
2) Divide between the sheets of baking paper, shape like cigars and roll up loosely. Twist the ends of the papers and steam in a covered pan for 20 minutes. Serve.

Refried Beans (Frijoles Refritos)

SERVES 4–6

400 g/14 oz/2 cups	canned pinto or black-eyed beans, drained and rinsed
3–4 x 15 ml spoons/ 3–4 tablespoons	vegetable oil

1) Fry the beans in the oil. Stir around with the back of a wooden spoon, pressing the beans together to form a cake. When a crust forms on the base, turn over and fry the other side. Serve.

Soup

Sopa de Fideos

Noodle soup, Mexican style. Less soupy than one might imagine, this is quite a substantial dish.

SERVES 4–6

	oil for deep-frying
175 g/6 oz/2 cups	egg noodles
2	onions, finely chopped
2	cloves garlic, crushed
1–2	Serrano chillies, deseeded and finely chopped
1	small green pepper, deseeded and chopped
200 g/7 oz/1 cup	passata (sieved tomatoes)
500 ml/18 fl oz/2 cups	vegetable stock
	salt and pepper
pinch	of brown sugar
5 ml spoon/1 teaspoon	dried marjoram or oregano

TO FINISH

chopped coriander (cilantro)

grated dry cheese such as Spanish Mahon or a grana e.g. Parmesan

1) Fry the noodles very briefly. Drain and set aside.
2) Pour off all but a couple of tablespoons of oil. Add the onions, garlic, chillies and pepper. Fry for a couple of minutes and add the noodles, passata and stock. Season to taste with salt and pepper.
3) Add the sugar and herbs. Simmer for 20 minutes, stirring from time to time.
4) Serve garnished with the coriander (cilantro) and cheese. Alternatively, send to the table with a good dollop of soured cream and a sprinkle of broken corn chips in each bowl.

Sopa de Arroz Rojos

Red rice 'soup' as opposed to the next recipe for green rice 'soup'! This is another of those 'dry soups' that are eaten as a first course. They are so filling that served with some cheese and a salad, I think they are a meal in themselves.

This dish can be started in a flameproof casserole on the top of the stove and then once the passata is added, bake at 180°C/350°F/Gas Mk 4 for 20 minutes.

SERVES 4–6

2 x 15 ml spoons/2 tablespoons	oil
200 g/7 oz/1 cup	rice
1	small onion, chopped
2	cloves garlic, crushed
1	Pasado chilli, crumbled
2.5 ml spoon/½ teaspoon	ground cumin
375 ml/13 fl oz/1½ cups	passata (sieved tomatoes)
125 ml/4½ fl oz/½ cup	water
100 g/3½ oz/½ cup	canned sweetcorn
1	red (bell) pepper, diced
	salt and pepper

1) Heat the oil. Cook the dry rice, stirring for 2 minutes.
2) Add the onion, garlic, chilli and cumin. Stir over a moderate heat for a couple of minutes.
3) Add the passata and water. Cover and cook for 10 minutes on a low heat. Add the sweetcorn and pepper and cook for a further 5 minutes. Season and serve.

Arroz Verde

Keeping the green theme, if you can find fresh tomatillos complete with their husks, use them to decorate this one-dish meal. Otherwise an extra sprinkle of coriander (cilantro) and some lime wedges will do.

SERVES 4–6

2 x 15 ml spoons/2 tablespoons	oil
200 g/7 oz/1 cup	rice
2 cloves	garlic, crushed
a bunch	of spring onions (scallions), chopped – including the green sections
1–2	Serrano chillies, deseeded and chopped
2.5 ml spoon/½ teaspoon	ground cumin
500 ml/18 fl oz/2 cups	vegetable stock
2 x 15 ml spoons/2 tablespoons	chopped flat parsley
2 x 15 ml spoons/2 tablespoons	chopped coriander (cilantro)
100 g/3½ oz/½ cup	peas – fresh or frozen
	salt and pepper

1) Fry the rice for a couple of minutes.
2) Add the garlic, spring onions (scallions), chillies and cumin. Cook for another couple of minutes then add the stock and the herbs.
3) Bring to the boil and simmer for 10 minutes. Add the peas. Cook for a further 3 minutes, season and serve.

Corn Soup

SERVES 4–6

2 x 15 ml spoons/2 tablespoons	oil
1	onion, chopped
2	canned Chipotle chillies, sliced
2 x 300 g/10 oz cans	creamed sweetcorn
	water
1	bay leaf
	salt and pepper

1) Fry the onion until golden. Add the chilli and fry for 1 minute.

2) Stir in the sweetcorn and enough water to give the consistency of single cream (half and half).

3) Add the bay leaf and season well with salt and pepper. Simmer for 10 minutes. Serve.

Sopa de Almendrada Verde

Have this soup hot or well chilled.

SERVES 4–6

225 g/8 oz/2 cups	potatoes, cubed
225 g/8 oz/1 cup	blanched almonds
2	green Serrano chillies, deseeded
4 x 15 ml spoons/4 tablespoons	flat parsley
1 clove	garlic, crushed
	water
	ice cubes (optional)

1) Boil the potatoes in salted water until tender.
2) Pour 250 ml/9 fl oz/1 cup of the water from the potatoes over the almonds in a liquidizer. Whizz until smooth. Scrape into a sieve and squeeze out as much liquid as possible.
3) Return this almond 'milk' to the cleaned out liquidizer with the potato, chillies, parsley, garlic and 500 ml/18 fl oz/2 cups of cold water. Whizz until well blended then strain through a fine sieve.
4) Season very well. Serve with an ice cube or two in prechilled bowls or reheat slowly and do not boil.

Gazpacho

There are many Spanish dishes which Mexicans have made their own. Gazpacho is one of them. Avocado and chilli are not found in most Old World recipes. This is a quick version. As with most chilled soups it would benefit from longer standing time to allow the flavours to develop. Ensure that all ingredients are chilled before you start and season well, then the speed won't matter too much.

This dish is quite substantial. Serve followed by some Nachos or Tostadas and most will be more than satisfied.

SERVES 4–6

750 ml/1¼ pints/3 cups	passata
2	crushed cloves garlic
4	spring onions (scallions), chopped
2	Serrano chillies, deseeded and finely shredded
½	a cucumber, peeled and chopped
	juice of a lime
2 x 15 ml spoons/2 tablespoons	olive oil
3 x 15 ml spoons/3 tablespoons	bread crumbs or crushed tortillas
2 x 15 ml spoons/2 tablespoons	chopped coriander (cilantro)
5 ml spoon/1 teaspoon	cumin
1	ripe avocado, peeled and diced

1) Whizz everything, except the avocado, in a blender in bursts until well mixed. Stir through the avocado and season to taste. Thin if necessary with a little more ice cold water.

2) You can serve with little bowls of chopped hard boiled eggs, olives, croutons, capers etc. for diners to add as desired.

Sopa de Lima

The best vegetable stock comes from celeriac and other aromatic roots such as carrots. Save the water when boiling these vegetables and freeze in ice cube trays. However, good fresh stocks are now available in supermarkets or, at a pinch, use vegetable bouillon powder.

SERVES 4–6

2 x 15 ml spoons/2 tablespoons	oil
1	onion, quartered
2 cloves	garlic
15 ml spoon/1 tablespoon	concentrated tomato purée
5 ml spoon/1 teaspoon	Caribe powdered chilli or New Mexico Red, if Caribe unavailable
1.25 litres/2 pints/5 cups	vegetable stock
	juice of 1½ limes
	soured cream (optional)
	coriander (cilantro) (optional)

1) Using a food processor, mince the oil, onion and garlic to a paste. Scrape out and fry until nicely browned.
2) Add the tomato purée and powdered chilli and fry, stirring until the mixture darkens.
3) Add the stock and simmer for 15 minutes. Add the lime juice. Season to taste and serve with a swirl of soured cream and a sprig of coriander (cilantro) if liked.

Sopa de Nopalitos

Cactus soup sounds a little odd but it is quite delicious.

SERVES 4–6

15 ml spoon/1 tablespoon	oil
4	onions, chopped
2 cloves	garlic, chopped
1	Jalapeño, chopped
1 x 350 g/12 oz jar or can	cactus pieces, drained, rinsed and cubed
1 litre/1¾ pints/4 cups	vegetable stock
2.5 ml spoon/½ teaspoon	dried oregano
a pinch	of dried rosemary
	salt and pepper
1	egg, lightly beaten
2 x 5 ml spoons/2 teaspoons	lime juice

1) Fry the onions, garlic and Jalapeño until softening. Add the cactus pieces and fry another 2 minutes. Add the stock and the herbs and season well. Simmer 15 minutes.

2) Put the egg and lime juice in a soup tureen. Add the soup by the ladleful, stirring continuously. Serve. If you need to reheat, do not boil.

Sopa Tascara

A creamy bean soup – this reminds me of Indian dhal, a roasted
chilli taking the place of the fried garlic.

SERVES 4–6

2 x 15 ml spoons/2 tablespoons	oil
2	onions, roughly chopped
2	Serrano chillies
2 cloves	garlic
2	carrots, chopped
1	stick celery, chopped
1	bay leaf
2	cloves
1 litre/1¾ pints/4 cups	water
	salt and pepper
400 g/14 oz can	pinto beans, rinsed and drained
6 x 15 ml spoons/6 tablespoons	crème fraîche
125 g/4 oz/1 cup	grated cheese – mild cheddar or Monterey Jack
2	Guajillo chillies, fried and chopped

1) Fry the onion and Serrano chilli for 3 minutes until browning.
   Add the garlic, carrot, celery, bay leaf and cloves. Fry, stirring,
   for another minute. Add the water and season well with salt
   and pepper. Boil for 15 minutes.
2) Purée the beans. Strain the water onto the beans. Simmer,
   stirring occasionally, for 5 minutes. Check seasoning. Serve
   with a spoon of crème fraîche stirred through each bowl and a
   sprinkle of cheese and Guajillo added at the last moment.

Sopa de Garbanzos

Not 'garbage soup' as my daughter misheard. Garbanzo is the Spanish name for chick pea. Epazote is the usual herb for this hearty soup but, unable to find it in Britain, I have used Winter Savory successfully to give a slightly bitter edge. However, as this is a herb reserved for home gardeners, I suggest using rosemary.

SERVES 4–6

15 ml spoon/1 tablespoon	oil
16	small strong onions, peeled and quartered – pickling onions are ideal
3 cloves	garlic, chopped
3	carrots, scraped and diced
1	leek, sliced
1 litre/1¾ pints/4 cups	vegetable stock or water
400 g/14 oz can	chick peas
a large sprig	of rosemary
	a bay leaf
	pepper
	salt
1	Chipotle chilli, fried and sliced
150 g/5 oz/¾ cup	crumbled feta cheese

1) Fry the onions, garlic, carrots and leek until browning.
2) Add the stock or water, chick peas, rosemary and bay leaf. Season with pepper. Simmer for 20 minutes. Season with salt.
3) Serve with the addition of a sprinkle of Chipotle and a spoon of cheese in each bowl.

Tortilla Soup

If you have time you can fry your own tortilla strips but packaged ones make quite a good substitute. Freeze dried chillies can also be used instead of frying your own but here there is a real difference in flavour.

SERVES 4–6

	oil
1	onion, chopped
2 cloves	garlic, crushed
500 ml/16 fl oz/2 cups	passata
1 litre/1¾ pints/4 cups	vegetable stock
2 x 15 ml spoons/2 tablespoons	chopped coriander (cilantro)
2 x 15 ml spoons/2 tablespoons	chopped mint
4	dried Ancho or Pasilla chillies
100 g/3½ oz/½ cup	Cheddar or Monterey Jack cheese, diced
1 x 150 g/5 oz packet	tortilla strips

1) Fry the onion, garlic and passata in 3 tablespoons of oil, stirring, for 5 minutes. Add the stock and chopped herbs. Season well and simmer.

2) Meanwhile fry the chillies in some hot oil until crisp – this will only take about half a minute. Drain and crumble.

3) Serve the soup and allow diners to sprinkle with the cheese, chillies and tortilla strips.

Salsas and Moles

Chiltomate

A very fiery, smooth tomato sauce from the Yucatán region. Traditionally it calls for epazote – pigweed or wormseed – but as that is very difficult for most cooks to source, I have omitted it and used a sprig of rosemary instead.

SERVES 4–6

2	Habanero chillies, deseeded
1	small onion
1 clove	garlic
400 g/14 oz can	chopped tomatoes
15 ml spoon/1 tablespoon	oil
the juice of 1	Seville orange – if unavailable use ½ an orange and ½ a lime
1 sprig	rosemary
	salt and pepper

1) Purée the chillies, onion, garlic and tomatoes until smooth in a food processor.
2) Fry the purée in the hot oil, stirring, for 5 minutes.
3) Add the orange juice, rosemary and a good pinch of salt and pepper.
4) Simmer on a minimum heat for another 5 minutes. Discard the rosemary and serve.

Guacamole

Guacamole is an avocado dip. In true Mexican cooking the avocado tends to be chopped rather than puréed. In TexMex it is sometimes mixed with soured cream. Although this may not be entirely authentic, it is delicious. There are many different ways to make Guacamole, so I have included three versions.

SERVES 4–6

1	small onion, very finely chopped
1–2	Serrano chillies, finely chopped
2	large ripe avocados, peeled and roughly chopped
	a good pinch of salt
	juice of half a lime
1	large tomato, skinned, seeded and diced
2 x 15 ml spoons/2 tablespoons	chopped coriander (cilantro)

1) Place the onion, chilli and avocado together in a bowl and mash with a fork. Mix in the salt, lime juice, tomato and coriander (cilantro), stirring well. Serve with tortilla chips or crudités.

Guacamole II

SERVES 4–6

2 large avocados
2 cloves garlic, crushed
juice of ½ a lime
salt and pepper
cayenne pepper
150 ml/5 fl oz pot soured cream (optional)

1) Whizz the avocados, garlic and lime in a food processor or liquidizer until smooth. Season to taste with salt, pepper and cayenne pepper.

2) Fold through the soured cream – if using. If you don't combine thoroughly you will be left with a marbled effect which is quite pretty.

Guacamole III

This guacamole is more in the vein of the Californian inspired salsa. Use it as a dip or as a salad dressing.

SERVES 4–6

1	small onion, finely chopped
2	cloves garlic, crushed
1–2	Serrano chillies, finely chopped
2	large avocados, peeled and diced
1	large tomato, skinned, seeded and diced
	juice of half a lime
2 x 15 ml spoons/2 tablespoons	chopped coriander (cilantro)
	olive oil
	salt and pepper

1) Mix together the onion, garlic, chillies, avocado, tomato, lime juice and coriander (cilantro). Add enough oil to give a runny consistency. Season with salt and pepper and serve.

Mole Oaxaqueño

This sauce from the Oaxaca region sounds rather curious but try it over Tamales (see page 6).

SERVES 4–6

2 x 15 ml spoons/2 tablespoons	oil plus extra if required
1	medium onion, chopped
2	cloves garlic, chopped
1	small bulb fennel, chopped
1	medium banana, diced
2 x 15 ml spoons/2 tablespoons	sesame seeds
2 x 15 ml spoons/2 tablespoons	raisins
2 x 15 ml spoons/2 tablespoons	ground almonds
2 x 15 ml spoons/2 tablespoons	bread crumbs
400 ml/14 fl oz/1¾ cups	passata
2.5 ml spoon/½ teaspoon	ground bay leaf
	a good grinding of black pepper
2 x 5 ml spoons/2 teaspoons	ground cinnamon
5 ml spoon/1 teaspoon	oregano
30 g/1 oz	plain chocolate, grated
4	Ancho chillies, soaked and puréed
15 ml spoon/1 tablespoon	wholefood peanut butter
125 ml/4½ fl oz/½ cup	water

1) Fry the onion, garlic, fennel and banana until softening. Remove with a slotted spoon and transfer to a food processor.
2) Add the sesame seeds, raisins, almonds and bread crumbs to the pan and fry gently until beginning to colour.
3) Add to the food processor with the passata, bay leaf, pepper, cinnamon, oregano and chocolate. Whizz until fairly smooth.
4) Fry the chilli purée adding a little more oil if required.
5) Stir in the contents of the food processor and add the peanut butter. Cook, stirring, for 2 minutes then add the water. Simmer for 10 minutes. Serve.

Mole Pepitas

Spoon this smooth pumpkin seed sauce over grilled vegetables or use it in the Yucatan speciality Papadzule (see page 63)

SERVES 4–6

2 x 15 ml spoons/2 tablespoons	oil
1	small onion, chopped
2 cloves	garlic, crushed
15 ml spoons/1 tablespoon	powdered Ancho chillies
60 g/2 oz/½ cup	toasted pumpkin seeds, finely ground
15 ml spoons/1 tablespoon	wholefood peanut butter
2 x 15 ml spoons/2 tablespoons	bread crumbs
a generous grinding	of black pepper
a good pinch	of salt
a pinch	of ground allspice
a pinch	of ground cloves
5 ml spoon/1 teaspoon	muscovado sugar
5 ml spoon/1 teaspoon	cinnamon
a pinch	of dried oregano
750 ml/1 pint 4 fl oz/3 cups	vegetable stock
15 ml spoon/1 tablespoon	butter

1) Fry the onion and garlic until soft and brown. Add the powdered chilli and cook, stirring, for 1 minute.

2) Place in a blender with the pumpkin seeds, peanut butter, bread crumbs and seasonings. Add only as much stock as is needed to process the mixture smoothly.

3) Scrape out and fry in the butter for 4 minutes, stirring constantly. Stir in the remaining stock and simmer for another 10 minutes.

Mole Poblano

Mole Poblano is a chilli sauce often enriched with chocolate. Usually meats are served in it. It can be used very simply over roasted vegetables or cornbread pudding. The choice of chocolate is very important. Most commercial brands are very sweet. Find a very dark plain one with at least 65% cocoa solids. There are specialist Mexican cooking chocolates available (see page x).

The ingredients list may seem a little daunting, but don't be put off, the method is simple and it won't take that long.

SERVES 4–6

3 x 15 ml spoons/ 3 tablespoons	sesame seeds
50 g/2oz/½ cup	ground almonds
75 g/3oz/½ cup	raisins
5 ml spoon/1 teaspoon	ground cinnamon
2.5 ml spoon/½ teaspoon	ground cumin
2.5 ml spoon/½ teaspoon	ground coriander (cilantro)
1.25 ml spoon/¼ teaspoon	ground black pepper
2.5 ml spoon/½ teaspoon	ground aniseed or fennel seeds
4	Mulato chillies, soaked, torn into pieces
4	Pasilla chillies, soaked, torn into pieces
4	Ancho chillies, soaked, torn into pieces
2	fresh red Cayenne chillies, chopped
1	large onion, roughly chopped
3 cloves	garlic, crushed
200 g/7 oz can	chopped tomatoes or passata
50 g/2 oz /1 cup	bread crumbs

2 x 15 ml spoons/2 tablespoons   oil
500 ml/18 fl oz/2 cups   vegetable stock
30 g/1 oz/1 heaped tablespoon   dark chocolate

1) Toast the sesame seeds in a dry frying pan (skillet). When just browning, stir in the almonds, raisins and spices. Stir around for half a minute then scrape into a blender or food processor.
2) Add the chillies, onion, garlic, tomato and bread crumbs. Process to a fairly smooth paste. If it is too heavy going add a tablespoon or two of the stock – no more though or it will be too sloppy.
3) Heat the oil in the pan over a low heat and fry the chilli paste for 5 minutes. Add the stock slowly. Then stir in the chocolate. Cook slowly for 15 minutes.

Mango Salsa

Part of the New Wave sweeping the Mexican resorts, mango salsa combines new ideas with traditional methods. Fruity and fragrant, it adds a fresh note to Burritos or Quesadillas (see pages 42 and 90).

SERVES 4–6

2	just-ripe mangoes, peeled and diced
1	small onion, chopped
1	Serrano chilli, finely chopped
2 x 15 ml spoons/2 tablespoons	coriander (cilantro), chopped
juice of ½	lime
1.25 ml spoon/¼ teaspoon	salt
a pinch	of brown sugar
a generous grinding	of black pepper

1) Mix everything together and serve.

Cook's Note
Green (under-ripe) mangoes can be used for a very tangy, crunchy salsa, but omit the lime juice and add a little more sugar.

Pepper Salsa

To grill (broil) the peppers, either place them in a naked flame or under a grill (broiler). When the skin has blackened and become papery it is very easy to remove.

SERVES 4–6

2	Jalapeño chillies, grilled, peeled and finely chopped
1	small red (bell) pepper, grilled, peeled and thinly sliced
1	small red onion, chopped
juice	of a lime
2 cloves	garlic, crushed
a good pinch	of salt
a small bunch	of fresh coriander (cilantro), chopped

1) Simply mix all the ingredients together. Allow to stand for 20 minutes before serving.

Quick Adobo

Use this sauce as a marinade – smear it on vegetables before grilling (broiling) or frying – or use a spoonful to perk up a soup or casserole.

MAKES 1 SMALL JAR

2 x 5 ml spoons/2 teaspoons	garlic purée
1 x 15 ml spoon/1 tablespoon	tomato purée
2 x 15 ml spoons/2 tablespoons	vinegar – cider or wine
1–2 x 5 ml spoons/ 1–2 teaspoons	Ancho chilli powder
5ml spoon/1 teaspoon	New Mexico Red chilli powder
pinch	of ground cloves
pinch	of ground cumin
2.5 ml spoon/½ teaspoon	ground cinnamon
1.25 ml spoon/¼ teaspoon	ground bay leaf
5 ml spoon/1 teaspoon	salt
a generous amount	of fresh ground black pepper

1) Simply mix all the ingredients together well. Store in a clean jar in the refrigerator.

Quick Red Onion Preserve

Red onion marmalades and preserves have been snatched up by New Wave cooks, but they aren't new. Mexicans were eating them for years. They are delicious with simple egg dishes or cheese.

MAKES 1 JAR

3	red onions, peeled and sliced
2 cloves	garlic, sliced
100 ml/3½ oz/a scant ½ cup	cider or white wine vinegar
15 ml spoon/1 tablespoon	water
2.5 ml spoon/½ teaspoon	crushed black peppercorns
2.5 ml spoon/½ teaspoon	salt
1.25 ml spoon/¼ teaspoon	ground cumin
2 x 15 ml spoons/2 tablespoons	caster (fine) sugar

1) Put everything except the cumin and sugar into a pan and bring to the boil. Simmer for 5 minutes.
2) Add the sugar, stir to dissolve then boil hard until thickened.
3) Pot and store in a cool place or use straightaway.

Cook's Note
Lime juice can be used instead of vinegar – use the juice of 1 lime topped up with water to make 100 ml/3½ fl oz/a scant ½ cup.

Salsa Cruda

Raw sauce! This is one of the simplest sauces you can make and you'll find yourself using it for all sorts of dishes, not just with Mexican food. Freshness is all. You can use a food processor to chop everything, but have a light hand on the pulse button – you don't want a purée.

SERVES 4–6

4	medium tomatoes – deseed and skin them, if liked – chopped
2	spring onions (scallions), chopped
2	Serrano chillies, chopped
2 x 15 ml spoons/2 tablespoons	chopped coriander (cilantro)
1.25 ml spoon/¼ teaspoon	salt
2.5 ml spoon/½ teaspoon	sugar
2 x 15 ml spoons/2 tablespoons	oil (optional)

1) Mix everything together, using the oil if the salsa is required for use as a salad dressing.

Tomato Sauce

This recipe has virtually the same ingredients as the previous salsa but this one is cooked briefly before serving.

SERVES 4–6

4	tomatoes, roughly chopped
4	spring onions (scallions), chopped
1–2 cloves	garlic, crushed
2	Serrano chillies, chopped
1.25 ml spoon/¼ teaspoon	salt
2.5 ml spoon/½ teaspoon	sugar
2 x 15 ml spoons/ 2 tablespoons	oil
2 x 15 ml spoons/2 tablespoons	chopped coriander (cilantro) or flat (Italian) parsley

1) Put everything except the oil and coriander (cilantro) or parsley into a food processor and whizz for a few seconds. Cook the paste in the oil until it thickens – about 5 minutes. Stir to avoid catching. Add the coriander (cilantro) or parsley and serve.

Xnipec

Xnipec or 'nose of the dog' is a very fiery sauce typical of the Yucatan region. Made with Habanero or Scotch Bonnet chillies and the local bitter oranges known as *mamey*, this salsa is not for the fainthearted – you have been warned! Use this as a serious challenge to those swaggering braggarts we all know, the ones who demand the ultimate chilli or the hottest vindaloo! If you cannot find Seville (bitter) oranges, use a blend of sweet orange juice with lemon or lime. If you prefer a less intimidating level of chilli heat, use a milder chilli.

SERVES 4–6

2	yellow Habanero chillies, finely chopped
2	small onions, finely chopped
1	large skinned and deseeded tomato, finely chopped
2 x 15 ml spoons/2 tablespoons	Seville (bitter) orange juice or see above
	salt to taste

1) Simply mix everything together and serve.

Cook's Note
Adding sugar is not authentic but it does temper the chillies' heat – but only slightly!

Main Courses

Burritos

Burritos are Northern Mexican fare, using wheat flour as opposed to corn tortillas.

MAKES 8

2 x 15 ml spoons/2 tablespoons	oil
2	onions, roughly chopped
1	Jalapeño chilli, chopped
1 clove	garlic, chopped
400 g/14 oz can	pinto beans, rinsed and drained
3	tomatoes, chopped
2 x 15 ml spoons/2 tablespoons	chopped coriander (cilantro)
	salt and pepper
8	wheat flour tortillas, warmed
350 g/12 oz/3 cups	grated Munster or Gouda cheese

1) Fry the onions and chilli in the oil until beginning to colour.
2) Add the garlic and beans. Crush the beans slightly whilst frying.
3) Add the tomatoes and coriander (cilantro). Cook stirring for 5 minutes. Season with salt and pepper.
4) Spread each tortilla with the bean mixture. Sprinkle thickly with cheese, roll up and serve immediately.

Baked Burritos

2 x 15 ml spoons/2 tablespoons	oil
2	onions, chopped
1	Jalapeño chilli, chopped
2 cloves	garlic, chopped
350 g/12 oz can	flageolet beans
150 g/5 oz/1 cup	peas, fresh or frozen
150 ml/5 fl oz/⅔ cup	soured cream
	salt and pepper
8	flour tortillas
300 g/10 oz/2½ cups	grated Munster or gouda cheese

1) Fry the onion and chilli until softened and add the garlic. Fry until colouring. Add the flageolet beans and peas. Stir around, then add the soured cream. Season well.

2) Divide between the tortillas and roll up. Put in a baking dish and cover with cheese. Bake at 200°C/400°F/Gas Mk 6 for 10 minutes. Serve.

Black Beans in Beer

SERVES 4–6

2	Ancho or Pasilla chillies, soaked and drained
4 cloves	garlic, crushed
1 bunch	spring onions (scallions), chopped
2 x 15 ml spoons/2 tablespoons	olive oil
1	medium onion, chopped
2 sticks	celery, finely sliced
1	carrot, finely diced
1	courgette (zucchini), diced
1	small red (bell) pepper, diced
1	small green (bell) pepper, diced
3	medium tomatoes, skinned and chopped
400 g/14 oz can	black beans
½	bottle Sol or similar Mexican beer
4	crisp corn tortillas
125 g/4 oz/1 cup	Cheddar or Monterey Jack, grated

1) Put the chillies, garlic, spring onions (scallions) and oil into a liquidizer and whizz to a paste.
2) Scrape into a heavy based pan and fry for 1 minute. Add the onion, celery, courgette (zucchini) and peppers. Fry for a couple of minutes then add the tomato and black beans. Cook for 1 minute then add the beer. Season with salt and pepper.
3) Layer the bean mixture with the tortillas into a heatproof dish. Scatter over the cheese and bake in a hot oven – 220°C/450°F/Gas Mk 8 – for 10 minutes. Serve.

Chiles Rellenos

Stuffed chillies, dipped in batter and then deep fried.

MAKES 6

6	Poblano chillies
2 x 15 ml spoons/2 tablespoons	butter
1	onion, chopped
2	large mushrooms, chopped
2.5 ml spoon/½ teaspoon	ground cumin
4 x 15 ml spoons/4 tablespoons	cooked rice or bread crumbs
175 g/6 oz/1 cup	mozzarella, diced
	salt and pepper
4	eggs, separated
2 x 15 ml spoons/2 tablespoons	flour
	oil

1) Grill (broil) the Poblanos until the skins are blackened. Peel, make a slit in the side and scrape out the seeds.
2) Fry the onion and mushrooms in the butter. When browned, add the cumin, rice or bread crumbs and cheese. Mix well and season.
3) Whisk the egg whites until stiff. Beat the yolks until pale. Fold into the whites with the flour.
4) Fill the Poblanos with the stuffing and then dip in the egg.
5) Deep fry in hot oil until crisp and golden. Serve immediately.

Cook's Note
The chillies can be filled with leftover Refried Beans (see page 7).

Black Bean Chilli Verde

This is a 'green' chilli. Serrano chillies are much hotter than Anaheim but Anaheim are much bigger – make your choice according to taste and the market.

SERVES 4–6

3	green peppers
2	Serrano or Anaheim chillies, deseeded
1 bunch	spring onions (scallions), chopped
5	tomatillos, if available
225 g/8 oz/4 cups	fresh spinach
2 x 15 ml spoons/2 tablespoons	vegetable oil
4 cloves	garlic, crushed
2	large cooking onions, roughly chopped
225 g/8 oz/2 cups	mushrooms
400 g/14 oz can	black beans, rinsed and drained – use Borlotti if black are unavailable
15 ml spoon/1 tablespoon	ground cumin
2 x 5 ml spoons/2 teaspoons	brown sugar
2 x 15 ml spoons/2 tablespoons	freshly chopped coriander (cilantro)

1) Grill (broil) the peppers (including the chillies) until the skins are black and papery.
2) Remove the blackened skin and the seeds and place in a food processor with the spring onions (scallions), tomatillos and spinach. Whizz to make a purée.
3) Fry the garlic and onions until browning. Add the mushrooms. Fry until the juices run.
4) Add the beans and the pepper purée. Cook, stirring.
5) Add the cumin and sugar. Simmer for 10 minutes. Stir in the coriander (cilantro) and serve.

Chard or Spinach Empanadas

Empanadas are turnovers, akin to Indian samosas. In fact, the dough is very similar. Traditionally they are deep fried but in this version they are baked in a hot oven for speed.

It is a bit of a sprint to make a dozen empanadas in 30 minutes but it is possible. An extra pair of hands when rolling and filling will speed you on your way.

MAKES 12

FILLING

15 ml spoon/1 tablespoon	oil, butter or vegetable margarine
1	small onion, chopped
2 cloves	garlic
1	Serrano chilli, finely chopped
2	tomatoes, chopped
250 g/9 oz/4½ cups	Swiss chard or spinach, washed, dried and cut or torn into strips
a good pinch	of ground allspice
	salt and pepper

DOUGH

	oil
200 ml/7 fl oz/¾ cup	boiling water
50 g/2 oz/¼ cup	soft butter or margarine
2.5 ml spoon/½ teaspoon	salt
350 g/12 oz/2½ cups	flour

1) Preheat the oven to 220°C/450°F/Gas Mk 8.

2) Fry the onion, garlic and chilli for a couple of minutes until softening.

3) Add the tomato and chard or spinach. Cook stirring from time to time until reduced and the liquid has been boiled off. Season with allspice, salt and pepper.

4) Put a couple of roasting tins in the oven with enough oil to cover the bottoms.

5) Place all the dough ingredients in a food processor with a dough attachment. Process until a soft dough is formed.

6) Divide into 12 balls. Roll each out to a tea plate size. Place a good spoon of the filling on one half. Fold over the dough to make a half-moon and pinch the edges together well.

7) Place all the turnovers in the hot oil and cook for 10 minutes, turning once, until browned and crisped.

Sweet Potato Empanadas

Use leftover cold sweet potatoes for these delicious parcels. If you haven't any, use ordinary cooked potato, carrots or even parsnips. To use raw sweet potatoes, peel, dice and cook quickly in a little boiling water until tender. You can do this whilst making the dough.

MAKES 12

FILLING

15 ml spoon/1 tablespoon	oil
1	small onion, finely chopped
1	Serrano chilli, finely chopped
15 ml spoon/1 tablespoon	ground almonds
15 ml spoon/1 tablespoon	raisins
300 g/10 oz/2 cups	cooked sweet potatoes, diced
5 ml spoon/1 teaspoon	ground cinnamon
	salt and pepper

DOUGH

	oil
200 ml/7 fl oz/¾ cup	boiling water
50 g/2 oz/¼ cup	soft butter or margarine
2.5 ml spoon/½ teaspoon	salt
350 g/12 oz/2½ cups	flour

1) Fry the onion and chilli for a couple of minutes. Add the almonds and raisins. Cook for a further minute.
2) Add the sweet potato and cinnamon and season well with salt and pepper.
3) Put all the dough ingredients into a food processor and work until a soft dough is formed.
4) Divide into 12 balls and roll each out to about an 18cm/7¼ in circle.
5) Place a spoon of filling on half and fold over, pinching the edges very well.
6) Deep-fry in batches until crisp and golden.

Cook's Note
These empanadas can also be baked as in the previous recipe.

Chilli Non Carne

This is a basic, very easy chilli, otherwise known in TexMex parlance as a bowl of red. Serve it with tortillas, rice or bread. Canned hominy grits or instant polenta also make good substantial foils for it. Serve with soured cream or cheese if liked.

SERVES 4–6

2 x 15 ml spoons/2 tablespoons	vegetable oil
225 g/8 oz/2 cups	mushrooms
2	medium onions, peeled and quartered
2 cloves	garlic, peeled
1	medium Poblano chilli, deseeded
400 g/14 oz	canned red kidney beans, rinsed and drained
400 g/14 oz	canned chopped tomatoes
	salt and pepper

1) Place the oil, mushrooms, onions, garlic and chilli into a food processor. Using the pulse button, chop until finely minced.
2) Scrape into a heavy frying pan (skillet). Fry over a high heat until browning.
3) Add the kidney beans. Cook for 2 minutes then add the tomatoes. Simmer for 10 minutes. Season and serve.

Chimichangas

A tasty way of using up Chilli leftovers. If you haven't any, use a mixture of cooked vegetables. Broccoli and sweetcorn with a dash of soured cream and a sprinkle of coarsely ground chilli powder is good.

Serve with a good dollop of soured cream, some shredded lettuce and Guacamole III (see page 27).

MAKES 6

400 g/14 oz/2 cups of leftover chilli or cooked vegetables
6 flour tortillas
oil for frying

1) Place a good spoon of the filling in the centre of each tortilla. Fold the bottom of the tortilla over the filling. Fold in the sides. Fold down the top to form a parcel. Secure with a cocktail stick (toothpick).
2) Heat the oil and fry until crisp and golden on both sides.

Enchiladas Suizas

Unctuous, utterly delicious and…fattening. Go on indulge your-self occasionally. Placate your conscience by filling up on lots of fresh salad vegetables.

MAKES 12

15 ml spoon/1 tablespoon	butter or oil
1	small bunch spring onions (scallions), chopped
2 cloves	garlic, chopped
375 g/12 oz/3 cups	mushrooms, preferably oyster and button, sliced
300 ml/10 fl oz/1¼ cups	crème fraîche
500 ml/18 fl oz/2 cups	passata
1	canned Jalapeño, chopped
4	tomatillos, chopped (use gherkins, if unavailable)
	salt and pepper
12	corn tortillas
	oil
175 g/6 oz/1 cup	mozzarella, torn into strips

1) Fry the spring onions (scallions), garlic and mushrooms briefly in the butter.
2) Add 60 g/2 oz/¼ cup of the crème fraîche and turn about.
3) Mix together the passata, Jalapeño, tomatillos and the remaining crème fraîche. Season.
4) Briefly fry the tortillas in the oil so they become pliable. Dip into the sauce, add a spoon of the mushroom mixture and roll up.
5) Lay in a lasagne dish and repeat, filling all the tortillas. Pour over the rest of the sauce. Cover with the mozzarella and bake at 200°C/400°F/Gas Mk 6 for 12 minutes. Serve immediately.

Enchiladas

Less rich than the Enchiladas Suiza (see page 54), this is a more run of the mill dish, but good. I have used aubergine (eggplant) strips instead of chicken, but you can use courgettes (zucchini), mushrooms, Quorn or whatever you fancy.

MAKES 12

2 x 15 ml spoons/2 tablespoons	oil
1	large aubergine (eggplant), cut into strips
2 cloves	garlic, crushed
2.5 ml spoon/½ teaspoon	ground cumin
75 ml/3 fl oz/⅓ cup	plain yoghurt or soured cream
	salt and pepper
1	onion, chopped
1 clove	garlic, chopped
2	Serrano chillies, chopped
1	small green (bell) pepper, chopped
1 x 400 ml/14 oz can	chopped tomatoes
12	corn tortillas
	oil
175 g/6 oz/½ cup	*chèvre sec* (aged goats' cheese) or if unavailable, feta, crumbled
2	spring onions (scallions), chopped (optional)

1) Fry the aubergine (eggplant) and crushed garlic in the oil. When browned and softened add the cumin and yoghurt or soured cream. Season.

2) In a separate pan, fry the onions, garlic, chillies and pepper then add the tomatoes. Cook over a high heat, stirring until slightly thickened.

3) Fry the tortillas very briefly.

4) Fill with the aubergine (eggplant) mixture, rolling up and placing them in a baking dish.

5) Cover with the tomato sauce, sprinkle with the cheese and cover tightly with foil. Bake at 200°C/400°F/Gas Mk 6 for 10 minutes.

6) Scatter the spring onions (scallions) over the enchiladas and serve.

Enchiladas with Sweet Potato

MAKES 12

2 x 15 ml spoons/2 tablespoon	oil
1	large sweet potato, peeled and diced
a bunch	of large spring onions (scallions) – green parts chopped, bulbs trimmed
2 cloves	garlic, chopped
1	lime
	salt and pepper
1–2	Jalapeño, finely chopped
450ml/15 fl oz/2 cups	passata
12	corn tortillas, steamed
125 g/4 oz/½ cup	dry ricotta or feta, crumbled

1) Fry the sweet potato, spring onions (scallions) and garlic until softened. Add the juice of the lime. Season.
2) Mix together the Jalapeño and passata.
3) Dip the tortillas in this mixture.
4) Fill with the sweet potato and lay in a baking dish. Pour over the remaining passata. Top with the cheese and bake for 10 minutes at 200°C/400°F/Gas Mk 6.

Fajitas

Fajitas actually means sashes. The term refers to the way the food (usually beef) is cut into strips. This recipe calls for aubergine (eggplant) but large flat mushrooms or courgettes (zucchini), even sweet (bell) peppers can be used.

MAKES 6

	2	medium aubergines (eggplants), halved and thinly sliced lengthways
	1	lime
15 ml spoon/1 tablespoon		plain flour
5 ml spoon/1 teaspoon		coarsely ground dried chilli
		oil
	6	large flour tortillas, warmed
	½	a tray of Roasted Peppers (see page 102)
	2	ripe avocados, peeled and sliced
	1	Serrano chilli, finely chopped
		coriander (cilantro)

plain flour and coarsely ground dried chilli } mixed together

1) Squeeze the lime juice over the aubergine (eggplant). Dust with the flour and chilli.
2) Fry in hot oil, in batches, until nicely browned.
3) Fill the tortillas with the aubergine (eggplant) and Roasted Peppers. Top with the avocado, sprinkled with the chopped chilli and a sprig of coriander (cilantro). Serve.

Flautas con Calabacitas

Courgettes (zucchini) are cut into strips before being rolled inside corn tortillas.

	MAKES 12
	oil
2 cloves	garlic, chopped
1	canned Jalapeño, sliced
450 g/1 lb/4 cups	courgettes (zucchini), in julienne
a pinch	of salt
a generous grinding	of black pepper
juice of ½	a lime
12	corn tortillas
3 x 15 ml spoons/3 tablespoons	grated Parmesan or Mahon cheese

1) Heat 2 tablespoons of oil in a pan, fry the garlic and chilli until the garlic colours. Add the courgette (zucchini) and stir fry until just tender – this does not take long.
2) Add salt and pepper and the lime juice.
3) Divide the mixture between the tortillas and roll up tightly to make fat cigars.
4) Fry in hot oil until crisp and golden. Dust with the cheese and serve with a chunky salsa.

Gorditas

Their name means 'little fatties' and they are a thicker tortilla. Almost like hoecakes, these cornmeal griddlecakes can be filled with most things from simple grated cheese to tomato sauces or use leftovers of Chilli (see page 52).

MAKES 12

150 g/5 oz/1 cup	instant polenta (pre-cooked cornmeal)
500 ml/18 fl oz/2 cups	water
2.5 ml spoon/½ teaspoon	salt
5 ml spoon/1 teaspoon	double acting baking powder
15 ml spoon/1 tablespoon	margarine
	oil
1	Serrano chilli, finely chopped
250 g/9 oz/1 cup	ricotta cheese
½	an Iceberg lettuce, shredded

1) In a non-stick pan cook the polenta, water, salt, baking powder and margarine over a low heat while stirring until the mixture leaves the pan sides easily. This takes only a few minutes.

2) Divide into 12 balls. Flatten each in turn on a sheet of baking paper and turn onto heated griddle or dry skillet. Cook turning until a crust develops on both sides.

3) Mix the chilli into the ricotta.

4) Heat the oil in a heavy frying pan or skillet. Fry the cornmeal cakes until golden and slightly puffed.

5) Drain and slit open. Fill with ricotta and lettuce. Serve immediately with a tomato salsa.

Mexican Lasagne

Here's another recipe for a baked dish. Like the Black Beans in Beer (see page 44), the tomato sauce is layered with tortillas. In some places this is known as *Budin*.

SERVES 4–6

3 x 15 ml spoons/3 tablespoons	oil
8	corn tortillas
1	onion, roughly chopped
2 cloves	garlic, chopped
a small can	tomatillos, drained and chopped – use a few gherkins if unavailable
750 ml/25 fl oz/3 cups	passata (sieved tomatoes)
2 x 15 ml spoons/2 tablespoons	chopped coriander (cilantro)
200 g/7 oz/1 scant cup	crème fraîche
175 g/6 oz/1 cup	mozzarella, torn
3	Pasado chillies, sliced or Anchoes, roasted and sliced

1) Fry the tortillas, reserve. Fry the onion, garlic and tomatillos. Add the passata. Stir around over a high heat for 2 minutes. Season and add the coriander (cilantro).

2) In deep heat proof dish lay a couple of tortillas. Cover with some of the tomato sauce, then some of the crème fraîche, the mozzarella and then a sprinkle of chillies. Repeat the layers until all is used up. Bake at 200°C/400°F/Gas Mk 6 for 20 minutes and serve.

Papadzules

Enchiladas from the Yucatan: these tortillas are filled with eggs and pumpkin seed sauce and dressed with Chiltomate, a fiery tomato sauce. Those of feebler temperament are advised to swap the Habanero chillies for something less hot.

MAKES 6

6 corn tortillas, steamed to warm
Mole Pepitas (see page 30)
6 hard-boiled (hard cooked) eggs, peeled and chopped
Chiltomate (see page 24)

1) Spread the tortillas with the Mole Pepitas, scatter over the hard-boiled (hard cooked) egg and roll up. Spoon over the Chiltomate and warm in a hot oven for 7–10 minutes at 200°C/400°F/Gas Mk 6. Serve.

Panuchos

This is another recipe from the Yucatan. The traditional method calls for a pocket to be made in the tortilla. Commercially available uncooked tortillas seem unwilling to open themselves up like this. Therefore these quick panuchos are a fried sandwich of two tortillas. I am relieved to discover from the authoritative *Authentic Mexican Cooking* by Rick and Deann Bayless that this is accepted practice in some places.

MAKES 6

	oil	
1	onion, chopped	
1	Serrano chilli, chopped	
400 g/14 oz can	black beans, rinsed and drained	
12	small thin corn tortillas	
2	hard-boiled (hard cooked) eggs, sliced	
3	tomatoes, peeled and chopped	} mixed
1	canned Jalapeño, thinly sliced	} together
1	cos (romaine) lettuce, shredded	
2 small jars	Italian Antipasti – cipolline in agrodolce and insalata di funghi	

1) Fry the onion and Serrano chilli in 4 tablespoons of oil. Add the beans and crush with the back of the spoon whilst stirring and frying.
2) Spread a good spoon of bean mixture on 6 tortillas. Top with the egg slices and then press a second tortilla on top.
3) Fry these tortilla sandwiches in oil, turning until golden on both sides.
4) Serve the tortillas garnished on top with a spoon of the tomato and chilli mixture, lettuce and the Italian onions and mushrooms.

Pepián

This is a creamy corn based stew. This version contains oyster (pleurot) mushrooms instead of the more usual pork. Serve with rice.

SERVES 4–6

4 x 15 ml spoons/4 tablespoons	oil
350 g/12 oz/4 cups	oyster (pleurot) mushrooms, cut in strips
2	onions, chopped
2	Pasado chillies, chopped
2 cloves	garlic, chopped
400 g/14 oz can	creamed sweetcorn
75 ml/2¾ fl oz/⅓ cup	evaporated milk plus extra if required
	salt and pepper
a bunch	of fresh coriander (cilantro), chopped

1) Fry the oyster (pleurot) mushrooms quickly in 2 tablespoons of the oil, until browned. Set aside.
2) Fry the onions and chillies in the rest of the oil until browning. Add the garlic. Fry for 1 minute. Add the sweetcorn and evaporated milk.
3) Turn heat right down. Season well with salt and pepper.
4) Simmer for 5 minutes, adding a little more evaporated milk if too thick. Add the mushrooms and coriander (cilantro). Simmer a couple of minutes longer and serve.

Tortilla Flats

See the recipe for Refried Beans (see page 7) or use canned variety.

MAKES 6

4 x 15 ml spoons/4 tablespoons	vegetable oil
600 g/21 oz/3 cups	Refried Beans
6 x 17.5cm/7in	flour tortillas
250 g/8 oz/2 cups	Double Gloucester or Monterey Jack cheese, grated
half	an Iceberg lettuce, shredded
2	ripe avocados, sliced
	Pepper Salsa or Salsa Cruda – homemade (see pages 35 and 38) or shop bought

1) Fry the beans in the oil, making 6 'cakes'.
2) Warm the tortillas in the oven.
3) Slide each bean 'cake' onto a tortilla. Scatter with cheese. Top with the lettuce, avocado slices and a spoon of salsa. Serve immediately.

Red Beans and Pepitas

Pepitas are in this instance pumpkin seeds. Find the smooth pale green ovals of shelled seeds in wholefood stores and delicatessens.

SERVES 4–6

125 g/4 oz/1 cup	pumpkin seeds, toasted
5 ml spoon/1 teaspoon	Ancho powder
5 ml spoon/1 teaspoon	Pasilla powder
15 ml spoon/1 tablespoon	ground cumin
15 ml spoon/1 tablespoon	muscovado sugar
2 x 15 ml spoons/2 tablespoons	oil
2	onions chopped
4 cloves	garlic, crushed
8 large (7.5cm/3in)	flat mushrooms
400 g/14 oz can	chopped tomatoes
200 g/7 oz can	sweetcorn kernels
bunch	of spring onions (scallions), chopped
400 g/14 oz can	Red beans, rinsed and drained
2 x 15 ml spoons/2 tablespoons	tomato purée ⎫ mixed
300 ml/½ pint/1 cup	hot water ⎭ together
	salt and pepper

1) Process the pumpkin seeds, reserving a handful for topping. When coarsely ground, mix together with the chilli powders, cumin and sugar.
2) Fry the onion, garlic and mushrooms. When browned, add the pumpkin seed mix. Stir around, then add the tomatoes, sweetcorn, most of the spring onions (scallions), leaving a handful for the top, the beans and the liquid.
3) Simmer for 10 minutes, adding more water if necessary.
4) Season to taste and top with the reserved seeds and spring onions (scallions).
5) Serve with flour tortillas or rice and a bowl of soured cream.

Tostadas

The toppings can be altered to accommodate what you have available. In this recipe, use canned Frijoles Refritos or your own leftovers (see page 7). As Tostadas are so simple and so good there are three variations on this theme. Try them all, then make up your own.

MAKES 12

15 ml spoon/1 tablespoon	oil
a good pinch	of cumin seeds
4	black peppercorns, crushed
1	bay leaf
	oregano
a small piece	of lime zest
	salt
1	red onion, sliced
2 cloves	garlic, sliced
1	canned Jalapeño chilli, chopped
175 g/6 oz/2 cups	sliced oyster (pleurot) mushrooms
2 x 15 ml spoons/2 tablespoons	water
12 x 10cm/4in	corn tortillas, fried crisp
400 g/14 oz/2 cups	Frijoles Refritos, reheated (see page 7)
150 ml/5 fl oz/¾ cup	crème fraîche
	coriander (cilantro)

1) Heat the oil, fry the cumin and peppercorns, then add the bay leaf, oregano, the lime zest, a good pinch of salt, onions, garlic, chilli and mushrooms. Cook quickly for 1 minute, then add the water and cook five minutes, until just tender.

2) Spread each tortilla with Refried Beans, top with the mushroom mixture and finish with a good spoon of crème fraîche and a sprig of coriander (cilantro).

Broccoli and Black Bean Tostadas

2 x 15 ml spoons/2 tablespoons	oil
a bunch	of spring onions (scallions), chopped
2 cloves	garlic, chopped
2	serrano chillies, chopped
2	large ripe tomatoes, chopped
400 g/14 oz can	black beans
2 x 15 ml spoons/2 tablespoons	chopped coriander (cilantro)
	salt and pepper
12 x 10cm/4in	corn tortillas, fried crisp
175 g/6 oz/3 cups	just cooked broccoli florets
	Guacamole II (see page 26) or 150 ml/5 fl oz/ soured cream and 1 large avocado, sliced
	dried chilli flakes (optional)

1) Fry the spring onions (scallions), garlic and chillies.
2) Add the tomatoes and black beans and cook until thick. Stir in the coriander (cilantro). Season.
3) Spoon onto the tortillas. Top with the broccoli and Guacamole or soured cream and avocado. Sprinkle with chilli flakes if liked. Serve.

Potato Tostadas

Unlike the two previous recipes there are no beans on these tostadas – their place is taken by a fragrant potato mixture similar to a curry.

MAKES 12

2 x 15 ml spoons/2 tablespoons	oil
2	Guajillo chillies, soaked
1	New Mexico Red chilli, soaked
1	onion, peeled and quartered
4 cloves	garlic, peeled
1	lime
a good pinch	of muscovado sugar
1.25 ml spoon/¼ teaspoon	salt
400 g/14 oz/2½ cups	potato, diced
2	tomatoes, diced
140 g/5 oz/1 cup	fresh or frozen peas
100 g/3½ oz/½ cup	sweetcorn kernels
12 x 10cm/4in	corn tortillas, fried crisp
150 g/5 oz/1 cup	crumbled dry goats' cheese or feta
1	Serrano chilli, finely shredded for garnish (optional)

1) In a food processor, mix the oil, Guajillo and New Mexico Red chillies, onion and garlic to make a paste.
2) Fry for 1 minute in a pan. Add the juice and a little grated zest of the lime. Stir in the sugar, salt, potatoes. Stir for about 1 minute. Add the tomatoes.
3) Cook covered until the potato is tender, adding a little water if necessary to prevent sticking.
4) Add the peas and sweetcorn and cook for another 3 minutes.
5) Spoon onto the corn tortillas. Top with the cheese and Serrano if using.

Blue Corn Aubergine (Eggplant) à la Veracruzana

This is a contrived dish in that Veracruzan sauce is more properly served with fish. There is an almost Mediterranean flavour to this dish. Blue corn is just another variety of ground maize, you can use ordinary golden cornmeal instead – the flavour will not suffer.

SERVES 4–6

1	very large or 2 medium aubergines (eggplants) – cut into 8 long slices
	salt
2 x 15 ml spoons/2 tablespoons	olive oil
2	medium onions, chopped
2 cloves	garlic, crushed
2	small green (bell) peppers, sliced
800 g/28 oz can	chopped tomatoes
75 g/2¾ oz/½ cup	green olives, chopped
75 g/2¾ oz/½ cup	capers
1	Jalapeño, sliced
15 ml spoon/1 tablespoon	coriander (cilantro), chopped
1	bay leaf
a good pinch	ground cloves
2.5 ml spoon/½ teaspoon	ground cinnamon
	black pepper
150 g/5 oz/1 cup	blue corn meal
	oil or butter to fry
1	lime

1) Sprinkle the aubergine (eggplant) slices with salt.
2) Fry the onion, garlic and green (bell) peppers for 5 minutes.
3) Add the tomatoes, olives, capers, Jalapeño, coriander (cilantro), bay leaf and spices. Season well with black pepper and salt.
4) Simmer for 15 minutes, stirring occasionally and adding a little water if the sauce becomes too thick and begins to stick.
5) Scrape the salt off the aubergines (eggplants).
6) Coat the slices both sides with cornmeal and shallow fry in hot oil until crisp and deep purple (nicely browned if using ordinary cornmeal).
7) Serve with the sauce and wedges of lime.

Eggs and Cheese

Chile Queso

Cheese stuffed chillies. The best chillies to use for this are Poblano but, as with the Chiles Rellenos (see page 45), if you can't bear things too hot, stuff a green (bell) pepper instead.

SERVES 4–6

6	Poblano chillies (see above)
300 g/10 oz/2 cups	mild feta cheese, crumbled
	a little oil
3	tomatoes, skinned and chopped
4 x 15 ml spoons/4 tablespoons	tortilla chips, crushed

1) Cut the chillies in half lengthways and remove the seeds. Fill with the cheese.
2) Pour a little oil into a shallow baking dish. Add the tomatoes and arrange the chillies on top, cut side up.
3) Sprinkle each with the tortilla crumbs and bake at 200°C/ 400°F/Gas Mk 6 for 20 minutes. Serve with tortillas or rice and an avocado salad.

Crepas con Elote

This is really a TexMex variant. Serve for breakfast, lunch or supper. Top with fillings if liked.

SERVES 4–6

4	eggs, separated
4 x 15 ml spoons/4 tablespoons	melted butter or margarine
300 g/10 oz can	creamed corn
250 ml/9 fl oz/1 cup	buttermilk or half and half milk and soured cream
300 g/10 oz/2 cups	cornmeal
2 x 5 ml spoons/2 teaspoons	bicarbonate of soda (baking soda) ⎫ sifted
5 ml spoon/1 teaspoon	salt ⎬ together
15 ml spoon/1 tablespoon	muscovado sugar ⎭
3	canned Jalapeño chillies, sliced
2	tomatoes, chopped
1	onion, finely chopped
	oil or butter to fry

1) Beat the egg yolks with the butter, creamed corn and buttermilk.
2) Whisk the egg whites until stiff. Combine all the ingredients gently.
3) Heat a little oil or butter on a seasoned griddle or heavy frying pan. Fry 7.5cm/3in pancakes, turning carefully to lightly brown both sides.

Chiles en Nogado

This dish of stuffed chillies is especially served on Independence Day. It has the colours of the Mexican flag: green, white and red. If you don't like things *muy piccante* use sweet green (bell) peppers instead.

SERVES 4–6

2 x 15 ml spoons/2 tablespoons	vegetable oil
2	large onions, finely chopped
2 cloves	garlic, crushed
2 x 15 ml spoons/2 tablespoons	raisins
2.5 ml spoon/½ teaspoon	ground cumin
120 g/4 oz/2 cup	bread crumbs
1	egg, beaten
	salt and pepper
4	large green chillies, halved lengthways and deseeded

EITHER

300 ml/½ pint/¼ cup *soured cream*

OR

300 ml/½ pint/1¼ cups *milk*
2 x 5 ml spoons/2 teaspoons *flour*
2 x 5 ml spoons/2 teaspoons *butter or margarine*

100 g/3½ oz/1 cup walnuts, chopped
1 pomegranate

1) Fry the onion and garlic in the oil. When golden, add the raisins, cumin and bread crumbs.
2) Remove from the heat, bind with the egg. Season with salt and pepper.
3) Press into the chilli halves and invert in a baking dish.
4) If using soured cream simply mix in the walnuts and spoon over. Otherwise whisk together the milk, flour and butter over a low heat until thickened.
5) Add the walnuts and pour over the chillies.
6) Bake at 200°C/400°F/Gas Mk 6 for 20 minutes. Top with the pomegranate seeds. Serve.

Entomatadas

Faster than the other two Enchilada recipes, this is much more of a TexMex variant, though it is found in the North of Mexico.

MAKES 12

1 x 400 ml/14 oz can	chopped tomatoes
1	onion, quartered
2 cloves	garlic, crushed
3	Serrano chillies
2 x 15 ml spoons/2 tablespoons	oil
12	corn tortillas
	oil
450 g/1 lb/4 cups	grated cheddar or Munster cheese

1) Whizz the tomatoes, onion, garlic and chillies until puréed.
2) Fry in the 2 x 15 ml spoons/2 tablespoons oil, stirring for 3 minutes. (Watch out for spattering.)
3) Fry the tortillas briefly to make them pliable.
4) Roll up with grated cheese inside – reserving some to sprinkle on the top.
5) Place in a shallow baking dish. Cover with the sauce. Add the cheese topping.
6) Cover with foil and bake at 200°C/400°F/Gas Mk 6 for 10 minutes. Serve.

Flautas con Queso Fresco

These crisp delicious tortillas tightly rolled with fresh cheese remind me of the Turkish Sigara Börek – often weirdly translated as cigarette pie! Eat the flautas (flutes) as snacks or make a Chiltomate sauce (see page 24) and pour it over the hot flautas and serve with a salad and/or Guacamole (see pages 25–27).

MAKES 12

12   corn tortillas

300 g/10 oz/1¼ cups   soft loose goats cheese or ricotta

oil

1) Lay out the tortillas. Place a line of cheese on each one. Roll up.
2) Heat the oil in a heavy frying pan or skillet. (You need a depth of 75mm/⅓ in of oil.) Fry the rolled tortillas, a few at a time, until crisp and golden. Serve.

Cook's Note
Chopped canned chillies, spring onions (scallions) or coriander (cilantro) can be added to the cheese before filling the tortillas.

Huevos Motuleños

In the original Mexican dish, ham is used. Here sun dried tomato strips give that salty tang.

SERVES 4–6

400 g/14 oz	canned chopped tomatoes
2–4	Serrano chillies, finely sliced
2 cloves	garlic, crushed
1	small onion, chopped
	vegetable oil
a pinch	of cumin
	salt
	sugar
6	tortillas
6	eggs
4	sun-dried tomatoes, cut into slivers
6 x 15 ml spoons/6 tablespoons	grated cheese or cottage/curd cheese

1) Process the tomatoes, chillies, and garlic briefly in a liquidizer or food processor.
2) Fry the onion in 2 x 15 ml spoons/2 tablespoons of oil. When lightly browned stir in the tomato mixture. Season to taste with the cumin, salt and sugar. Simmer until thickened.
3) Fry the tortillas and keep warm.
4) Fry the eggs adding the sun-dried tomato shards at the last moment.
5) Place the eggs on the tortillas. Cover with the sauce and top with the cheese. Serve.

Huevos Rancheros

Fried eggs Mexican style. Use either your own pepper salsa or a good commercially prepared one.

SERVES 1

vegetable oil

1 small tortilla per person

1 egg per person

1–2 x 15 ml spoons/
1–2 tablespoons Hot Pepper Salsa (see page 35) per person

1) Fry the tortillas in the oil and keep warm in the oven.
2) Fry the eggs. Place an egg on each tortilla and serve topped with the Hot Pepper Salsa.
3) Decorate if liked with fresh coriander (cilantro) and/or avocado.

Huevos Revueltos

Scrambled eggs but 'estilo mexicano' (Mexican-fashion). Eat these tasty eggs for breakfast, lunch or supper. Roll them up in soft tortillas or serve with crusty rolls.

SERVES 4–6

75 g/2¾ oz/⅓ cup	butter or white vegetable fat
1	onion, chopped
2 cloves	garlic, chopped
1	Jalapeño chilli, chopped
1	large tomato, seeded and chopped
8	eggs, lightly beaten
	salt and pepper

1) Melt the fat in a large skillet. Fry the onion, garlic, chilli and tomato for a few minutes. Stir in the eggs and season. Keep stirring until the eggs are just set then serve immediately.

Mexican Cheese on Tortilla

Almost as quick as cheese on toast, this recipe uses flour tortillas and ready-made sauces. You can of course use your own salsa (see pages 24–40) but this will increase the time taken.

SERVES 4–6

1	Serrano chilli, chopped
225 g/8 oz/2½ cups	mushrooms, chopped
1 x 15 ml spoon/1 tablespoon	oil
3	large flour tortillas
225 g/8 oz/2 cups	Monterey Jack or mild Cheddar, grated
1 jar	pepper salsa

1) Fry the chilli and mushroom in the oil.
2) Scatter over the tortillas and sprinkle with the cheese.
3) Bake in a hot oven – 230°C/450°F/Gas Mk 8 – for 8 minutes or until the edges are crisp. Serve, cut into wedges, with a spoon of salsa.

Mexican Corn Pudding

a small	stale loaf, cubed
400 g/14 oz can	sweetcorn
2	large eggs, beaten
125 ml/4½ fl oz/½ cup	milk
	salt and pepper
2	canned Jalapeño chillies, finely chopped
2	spring onions (scallions), sliced
30 g/1 oz/¼ cup	finely grated cheese

1) Mix together the bread, sweetcorn, eggs and milk. Season with salt and pepper. Add the chillies and spring onions (scallions).
2) Pour into a greased flat baking dish.
3) Sprinkle with the cheese and bake in a moderate oven – 180°C/375°F/Gas Mk 4 for 20 minutes. Serve cut into squares with a Hot Pepper Salsa (see page 35).

Nopales and Egg

This is another version of Huevos Revueltos (see page 86). If you cannot get nopales – cactus stems – use steamed broccoli stems with a squeeze of lime juice. Not the same but still tasty.

SERVES 4–6

2 x 15 ml spoons/2 tablespoons	oil or butter
1	onion, chopped
1	canned Jalapeño chilli, cut into thin strips
1	tomato, roughly chopped
1 x 350 g/12 oz jar or can	cactus pieces – empty into a sieve and run under the tap for a minute then slice
8	eggs, lightly beaten with a little salt

1) Fry the onion and chilli. Add the tomato and cactus pieces. Cook until softened then add the eggs and stir around until just set. Serve immediately with warm tortillas.

Quesadillas

SAUCE

2 x 5 ml spoons/2 teaspoons	Ancho powder
200 g/7 oz tin	chopped tomatoes
1	small onion, roughly chopped
2 cloves	garlic, crushed
15 ml spoon/1 tablespoon	oil
a good pinch	of muscovado sugar
	salt and pepper
15 ml spoon/1 tablespoon	chopped parsley
a squeeze	of lime
4	flour tortillas
150 g/5 oz/1¼ cups	crumbled feta cheese
4	spring onions (scallions), chopped
a little	oil

1) Place the Ancho powder, tomatoes, onion and garlic in a liquidizer or processor and whizz briefly.
2) Fry the paste in the oil for 5 minutes, stirring. Add the sugar, and season with salt and pepper. Add the parsley and lime.
3) Spread a spoon of the tomato sauce over half a tortilla. Cover with cheese and spring onion (scallion). Fold over to make a half moon shape and fry in a very little oil on both sides.
4) Cut into triangles to serve.

Cook's Note
Bottled sauces can be used for speed. If liked, try with Munster or Mozzarella cheeses (diced finely).

Queso Fundido

Queso fundido is essentially melted cheese like in a Swiss or French fondue – indeed if you have a fondue set you can melt the cheese carefully over the spirit burner at the table. Widely available cheeses have been substituted for the authentic Mexican ones but if you live near an esoteric deli, try asking for *Queso de Oaxaca* or *Queso de Chihuahua*.

SERVES 4–6

2	Ancho (dried Poblano) chillies, dry roasted and crumbled
3	spring onions (scallions), chopped
15 ml spoon/1 tablespoon	coriander (cilantro), chopped
375 g/12 oz/2 cups	cubed cheese – a mixture of two or more of the following: mozzarella, Munster, Greve, Monterey Jack, Cheshire
8	corn or flour tortillas

1) Mix together the Anchos, spring onions (scallions) and coriander (cilantro).
2) Melt the cheese in a heatproof dish in a moderate oven until bubbling.
3) Sprinkle with the chilli mixture and serve.
4) Diners scoop out cheese and roll it up in tortillas to eat – messy but delicious. Serve with a fresh salsa and some oven-roasted peppers, tomatoes and courgettes (zucchini).

Vegetables and Salads

Ejote con Tortilla

Beans aren't the only vegetables you could use for this very simple dish: cauliflower, broccoli, courgettes (zucchini) and mangetout all work well.

SERVES 4–6

2 x 15 ml spoons/2 tablespoons	oil
2 cloves	garlic, crushed
1	small onion, chopped
1	Serrano chilli, deseeded and finely chopped
500 g/1 lb 2 oz/6 cups	green beans, cut into 2.5cm/1in lengths
125 ml/4 fl oz/½ cup	water or tomato juice
	salt and pepper
a pinch	of sugar
2 x 15 ml spoons/2 tablespoons	chopped coriander (cilantro)
2 x 15 ml spoons/2 tablespoons	broken tortilla chips

1) Fry the garlic and onions. Add chilli and beans. Cook, covered for a couple of minutes over a moderate heat, shaking the pan occasionally.

2) Pour in the water or tomato juice. Season with salt, pepper and a pinch of sugar.

3) Cover and cook slowly until the beans are tender – about 10 minutes.

4) Stir through the coriander (cilantro) and sprinkle over the crushed tortilla chips. Serve immediately.

Elote

This is simply corn on the cob. When next barbecuing, throw some sweetcorn on the grill rack and serve in this way.

SERVES 4–6

6	sweetcorn on the cob
1	lime, cut into wedges
50 g/2 oz	butter
2.5 ml spoon/½ teaspoon	dried crushed red chillies
a good pinch	of salt

1) Boil the corn in plenty of *unsalted* water for 7 minutes. Drain.
2) Rub each corn with a wedge of lime. Serve with the butter and sprinkle with the chilli and salt.

Cook's Note
If you have time work the chilli and salt into the butter. Chill well then serve cut into pats with the corn.

Ensalada à la Mexicana

This is really Mexico through US eyes as salad south of the border is more like a chutney or relish. However questionable its antecedents, this is a great salad. The vinaigrette is fiery. If you want to temper its heat, choose a milder chilli.

SERVES 4–6

1	large cos (romaine) lettuce, shredded
a small bunch	of rocket (arugula)
90 g/3 oz/1½ cups	coriander (cilantro)
150 g/5 oz/1 cup	radishes, sliced
2	Habanero chillies, quartered and deseeded
a small bunch	of spring onions (scallions), roughly chopped
350 g/12 oz can	tomatillos, rinsed and drained
200 ml/7 fl oz/¾ cup	good corn or olive oil
	juice of 1 lime
2 x 15 ml spoons/2 tablespoons	light muscovado sugar
100 ml/3½ fl oz/⅓ cup	of boiling water
1	small red onion, finely chopped
2	corn tortillas, fried crisp and crumbled
90 g/3 oz/½ cup	feta cheese, crumbled

1) Mix together the cos (romaine), rocket (arugula), coriander (cilantro) and radishes and place on a salad plate.
2) Put the chillies, spring onions (scallions) and tomatillos in a food processor and chop to a very rough purée with the pulse button. Add the oil, lime juice, sugar and boiling water and whizz at a high speed for a few seconds.
3) Pour over the salad. Sprinkle with the red onion, tortilla crumbs and the feta. Serve immediately.

Ensalada de Aguacate

Avocado salad with a kick. Use this salad as a side dish or use it to stuff flour tortillas with a handful of crumbled feta cheese.

SERVES 4–6

½	an Iceberg lettuce, shredded
3	ripe avocados, peeled and sliced
2 x 15 ml spoons/2 tablespoons	chopped coriander (cilantro)
1–2	Guajillo chillies, dry roasted and crumbled
1 cloves	garlic, crushed
1	small onion chopped
	salt and pepper
	oil

1) Line a salad dish or plate with the lettuce. Cover with the avocado slices.
2) Mix together the coriander (cilantro), chillies, garlic and onion. Sprinkle over the salad. Season then drizzle with oil to taste.

Hongos à la Mexicana

Mexican mushrooms, well...mushrooms in a Mexican style. This is good with soft corn or wheat flour tortillas to mop up those gorgeous juices.

SERVES 4–6

2	fresh Poblano chillies, halved and seeded
2 x 15 ml spoons/2 tablespoons	oil
2	onions, chopped
2 cloves	garlic, chopped
750 g/1½ lbs/6 cups	big dark mushrooms, cut into chunks
15 ml spoon/1 tablespoon	chopped celery leaves or use celery salt to season
500 ml/18 fl oz/2 cups	passata
a sprig	of thyme
2.5 ml spoon/½ teaspoon	dried oregano
a sprig	of rosemary
1	bay leaf
	salt and pepper
250 ml/9 fl oz/1 cup	water or vegetable stock

1) Grill (broil) the poblanos until the skins blacken. Cool a little, peel and chop roughly.
2) Fry the onion and garlic. When browning, add the mushrooms. Cook stirring over a fairly high heat for 5 minutes. Add the celery leaves and passata. Cook for 4 minutes, stirring.
3) Add the remaining ingredients, seasoning well. Simmer until thick. Serve.

Jícama Salad

Jícama looks like a pale brown beetroot and has a crisp flesh. It makes a lovely, juicy and refreshing salad – celeriac can be substituted if required.

SERVES 4–6

1	cos (romaine) lettuce
about 500 g/1 lb	jícama, peeled and sliced into half-moons
1	medium papaya, peeled, halved and deseeded and sliced
1	cucumber, halved lengthways, deseeded and sliced
2	spring onions (scallions), chopped

DRESSING

the rind and juice of 1	lime
4 x 15 ml spoons/4 tablespoons	oil
1 crushed clove	garlic
a good pinch	of salt
a pinch	of sugar
1	dried Pequín chilli, crumbled or chopped

1) Line a bowl or salad plate with the lettuce leaves. Arrange the jícama, papaya and cucumber slices over the lettuce. Scatter over the spring onions (scallions). Shake the dressing ingredients together in a screw topped jar and pour over the salad. Serve.

Pattypan Squash

If you can get the baby squashes, use them whole. If no pattypan are available, use other types of squash including marrow, courgette (zucchini), butternut and pumpkin. Serve with rice and grated cheese as a full meal or use as a side dish or tortilla filling.

SERVES 4–6

2 x 15 ml spoons/2 tablespoons	vegetable oil
1	large onion, chopped
3 cloves	garlic, crushed
2	Serrano chillies, deseeded and finely shredded
500 g/1 lb/4 cups	pattypan squash, cut into 2.5cm/1in chunks
3	large tomatoes, chopped or 200 g/7 oz canned chopped tomatoes
1	green (bell) pepper, deseeded and chopped
	salt and pepper

1) Fry the onion and garlic until softening. Add the rest of the ingredients. Fry stirring over a moderate heat for 5 minutes then cover tightly.
2) Turn to low and cook a further 15 minutes.
3) Season with salt and pepper. If liked, add a handful of chopped coriander (cilantro) or parsley just before serving.

Cook's Note
This dish is equally good hot, tepid or well chilled.

Roasted Peppers

This dish is very similar to the Spanish *Esclavida*. If you happen to be barbecuing, roast the peppers over the coals otherwise crank the oven temperature up as high as it will go.

SERVES 4–6

3	Poblano chillies, deseeded
3	Serrano chillies, deseeded
2	sweet red (bell) peppers
1	yellow (bell) pepper
1	green (bell) pepper
4	small onions, peeled and trimmed
4 cloves	garlic
	oil
	coarsely ground salt
	freshly ground black pepper
a sprig	of thyme
5 ml spoon/1 teaspoon	dried oregano
150 ml/5 fl oz/a heaped cup	crème fraîche

} quartered and deseeded (for the red, yellow and green peppers)

1) Place all the chillies and peppers on a heavy-duty baking tray with the onions and garlic. Drizzle over the oil. Sprinkle liberally with salt and pepper.
2) Bake in the hottest oven you can manage until blackened and soft – about 15 minutes.
3) Peel off the skins and roughly cut into chunks. Add the herbs and crème fraîche. Reheat and season if necessary.
4) Eat with soft tortillas or crusty rolls.

Snacks

Devilled Nuts

Much nicer than commercially available dry-roasted peanuts, these nuts are sold on the street in many Mexican cities. Use whichever nuts you like or have to hand. Pecans – natives of Mexico – and almonds are especially good. Seeds, such as pumpkin or sunflower, can also be used as can soy bean 'splits' (toasted soy beans sold as snack food).

SERVES 4–6

150 g/5 oz/1 cup	shelled peanuts
5 ml spoon/1 teaspoon	ground chilli
a good pinch	of salt

1) Dry roast the peanuts, shaking the pan to toast them evenly. Sprinkle over the chilli and salt. Shake for a few more seconds to evenly coat the nuts and serve when cooled.

Cook's Note
If liked, a few drops of lime juice can be squeezed over the nuts.

Jícama

Jícama is a root vegetable, with the shape of a large Christmas bauble. It looks like a pale brown skinned beet. The flavour is slightly sweetish, slightly fruity. If you are unable to find it, a good substitute for these crudités is celeriac – the turnip-rooted celery.

SERVES 4–6

375 g/12 oz/2 cups	jícama, peeled and cut into thin batons
	juice of a lime
2 x 5 ml spoons/2 teaspoons	coarse sea salt } mixed
2.5 ml spoon/½ teaspoon	coarsely ground cayenne pepper } together

1) Arrange the jícama on a plate. In the middle, place a deepish saucer. Put the lime juice in the middle of the saucer and sprinkle the salt and cayenne around the edge. Diners dip the batons first in the lime juice and then in the salt and cayenne.

Nachos

400 g/14 oz can	refried beans or see page 7
1 large packet	Tortilla corn chips
2	medium tomatoes, peeled, seeded and diced
225 g/8 oz/2 cups	Monterey Jack or Cheddar cheese, grated
2–3	canned Jalapeños, thinly sliced

1) Heat the beans then spread a little on each tortilla chip.
2) Lay out on a baking (cookie) sheet.
3) Scatter over the tomato and cheese and top with a few slices of
   Jalapeño. Heat for a few minutes at 200°C/400°F/Gas Mk 6,
   until the cheese is bubbling and serve immediately.

Nopales Nibbles

A friend reports munching on nopales in a Mexican equivalent to a Tapas bar. Serve this snack also as a side dish or salad.

SERVES 4–6

2 x 15 ml spoons/2 tablespoons	oil
1	onion, finely chopped
1	Jalapeño, chopped
2 cloves	garlic, crushed
350 g/12 oz can or jar	cactus pieces, drained, rinsed and cubed
	salt and pepper
1	lime (optional)

1) Fry the onion, chilli and garlic until softening but not colouring.
2) Add the cactus pieces, tossing like a salad to coat in the fragrant oil. Season with salt (go easy), pepper and a squeeze of lime if liked. Serve warm or cold.

Quick Sopes

This is a cheat's version of a favourite Mexican snack. It preserves the idea of the dish but not its rather involved labour-intensive production. The secret is to use a cast iron muffin or popover pans and to preheat them and the oven.

Don't be put off by the length of the ingredients – just choose one from the filling list and a couple from the toppings. It is a great way of using up leftovers and the scooped out middles of the sopes can be used as dumplings in a soup or stew. Simply cool and pop into a bag and store in the freezer until required.

MAKES 18

oil

115 g/4 oz/¾ cup	cornmeal	
115 g/4 oz/¾ cup	plain flour	sifted
5 ml spoon/1 teaspoon	baking powder	together
2.5 ml spoon/½ teaspoon	salt	
2	eggs	
285 ml/10 fl oz/1⅓ cups	milk	

FILLINGS

Refried Beans, reheated (see page 7)

Huevos Revueltos, reheated (see page 86)

leftover chilli, reheated

chopped avocado and fresh chilli

ricotta cheese

(You'll need enough to fill 18 sopes – about 1 tablespoon each.)

TOPPINGS

1 jar   cactus or tomato salsa
        shredded lettuce
        radish slices
        coriander (cilantro)

1) Pour a little oil into the bases of an 18–hole muffin tray (or use 2 x 9-hole trays). Put in a hot oven – 220°C/450°F/Gas Mk 8 – to heat.
2) Using a large whisk beat the eggs and milk into the cornmeal and flour mixture. Fill the muffin trays two-thirds full.
3) Bake 15 minutes until well risen and golden.
4) Turn out and scoop out the centres of the sopes with a melon baller. Do not scoop through the base. Reserve the middles for later use.
5) Fill the resulting cases with one of the fillings and add your chosen toppings. Serve immediately.

Tostaditas con Elote

This is such an easy dish to throw together. You can alter it by using Guacamole III (see page 27) instead of the tomato mixture. If you are in a hurry choose a good quality ready-made tomato salsa. The colours are part of its charm – if you can find the rare blue corn tortillas, so much the better.

SERVES 4–6

4	large tomatoes
2	spring onions (scallions), chopped
4	tomatillos, fresh or canned, chopped
2 x 15 ml spoons/2 tablespoons	chopped coriander (cilantro)
	salt and pepper
15 ml spoon/1 tablespoon	melted butter
1	canned Jalapeño, thinly sliced
400 g/14 oz/2 cups	sweetcorn, canned or frozen
12	small corn tortillas, fried crisp
150 ml/5 fl oz/⅔ cup	crème fraîche
1	Serrano chilli, finely sliced – optional

1) Blacken the tomato skins – either in a gas flame or under a hot grill (broiler) – and remove. Chop. Mix in the spring onions (scallions), tomatillos and coriander (cilantro). Season with salt and pepper.

2) Fry the Jalapeño and sweetcorn in the butter for 3 minutes.

3) On each tortilla place a layer of sweetcorn, a spoon of the tomato mixture, a teaspoon of crème fraîche and a slice of Serrano. Reheat very briefly on a baking sheet. Serve.

Pico de Gallo

Pico de gallo is found at roadside stalls and snack bars but it makes a delicious appetiser or starter. It's perfect at a barbecue or an *al fresco* meal.

SERVES 4–6

¼ of a watermelon, cubed

2 jícama, peeled and cubed

1 cucumber, cubed

4 small oranges, peeled and cut into eighths

4 apples, cored and cut into chunks

1 small pineapple, peeled and cubed

juice of 1 lime

a few mint leaves

1) Mix everything together and serve with a jar of toothpicks for diners to spear their chosen chunks.

Cook's Note
Avocado can also be added.

Desserts and Sweets

Atole de Almendrada

Eat this cornmeal porridge for breakfast or as a homely comforting pudding.

Authentically it is made with more water and used as a thick drink. My husband likened it to drinking knitting!

SERVES 4–6

30 g/1 oz/a scant ¼ cup	instant polenta
15 ml spoon/1 tablespoon	ground almonds
250 ml/9 fl oz/1 cup	water
250 ml/9 fl oz/1 cup	milk
5 ml spoon/1 teaspoon	ground cinnamon
2–4 x 15 ml spoons/ 2–4 tablespoons	muscovado sugar

1) Mix everything together well and stir over a moderate heat until the mixture thickens. Cook for 3 minutes. Serve.

Baked Tree Tomatoes

Tree Tomatoes or *Tomate de arbol* are more commonly found commercially labelled as Tamarillos. This is the name ascribed to them by the New Zealand growers; they are, however, natives of Central and South America. They can be eaten raw but the fruit is sharply acidic. Baked, the flavour mellows and the colour deepens.

SERVES 4–6

6	tamarillos, peeled and halved	
4 x 15 ml spoons/4 tablespoons	brown sugar	} mixed
2 x 5 ml spoons/2 teaspoons	ground cinnamon	} together
25 g/1 oz/¼ cup	butter	

1) Place the tamarillos in a baking dish, cut-side up.
2) Sprinkle thickly with the sugar and cinnamon.
3) Dot with butter and bake in a moderate oven – 180°C/350°F/Gas Mk 4 – for 20 minutes.

Cabellero Pobre

Mexican bread and butter pudding is usually flavoured with cinnamon and raisins. To cut down on preparation time, this recipe uses the commercially available Cinnamon Raisin breads.

SERVES 4–6

250 ml/9 fl oz/1 cup	full cream milk, warmed to just below a simmer
4 x 15 ml spoons/4 tablespoons	sugar
a few drops	vanilla essence
a	small Cinnamon and Raisin Loaf, cut into cubes
	zest of an orange
3	eggs, beaten

1) Mix everything together very well.
2) Pour into a well-greased baking dish and bake in a moderate oven – 180°C/350°F/Gas Mk 4 – for 25 minutes.

Calabaza en Tacha

Pumpkin in syrup! This is a Christmassy dish that can be eaten warm or chilled. You can bake or boil this simple but intriguing mixture. Serve with Flan (see page 122), cream or custard. If you can't get sloes, use 15 ml spoon/1 tablespoon dried blueberries or simply omit this ingredient.

SERVES 4–6

225 g/8 oz/1 cup	golden granulated or light brown sugar
250 ml/9 fl oz/1 cup	water
2 x 15 ml/2 tbs	cider vinegar or lime juice
2 sticks	of cinnamon
2	cloves
a long strip	of orange zest
500 g/1 lb/4 cups	pumpkin, cubed
2	guavas, peeled and cubed
1	orange, peeled and segmented
15 ml spoon/1 tablespoon	sloes

1) Melt the sugar in the water and vinegar or lime juice.
2) Add the spices and orange zest and bring to the boil. Cook for 3 minutes then add the remaining ingredients.
3) Simmer gently or bake until the pumpkin and guava is tender – about 20 minutes.

Chocolate Cream

You can eat this grainy pudding warm or well chilled with a swirl of cream and a sprinkle of ground cinnamon.

Use a heavy bottomed pan and a low flame or a double boiler.

SERVES 4–6

175 g/6 oz/1 cup	dark chocolate, grated or in chips
1 litre/1¾ pints/4⅓ cups	full cream milk
5 ml spoon/1 teaspoon	finely grated orange rind
5 ml spoon/1 teaspoon	ground cinnamon
15 ml spoon/1 tablespoon	dark rum
60 g/2 oz/⅓ cup	light muscovado sugar
2	egg yolks
2 x 15 ml spoons/2 tablespoons	cornmeal

1) Melt the chocolate in half the milk, the orange rind and the cinnamon.
2) Stir in the rum. Add the sugar and stir well.
3) Beat the egg yolks with the cornmeal and pour on the chocolate mixture. Beat in the remaining milk. Cook, stirring, until well thickened.
4) Serve immediately or set in small bowls in a cool place until well chilled.

Chongos

This is what Señorita Muffita would eat in Mexico before the tarantula comes down and really frightens her away – Chongos are curds and whey and instead of rennet, lime juice is used to form the curds. Some places add eggs to the mixture making it more like a posset than a junket. This pudding takes no time to make but improves with standing in a cool place before serving.

SERVES 4–6

750 ml/1 pint 7 fl oz/3 cups	full cream milk, warmed to 37°C/98°F
4 x 15 ml spoons/4 tablespoons	caster sugar
2 x 5 ml spoons/2 teaspoons	ground cinnamon
	the juice of 1 lime

1) Combine the milk with 3 tablespoons of the sugar and 1 teaspoon of cinnamon.
2) Slowly stir the lime juice into the milk, don't whisk it or the curd will be all broken up. Pour into a chilled dish and put in the refrigerator before serving. Sprinkle with the remaining sugar and cinnamon mixed together before sending to the table.

Cook's Note
Rosewater is sometimes added to the milk for flavour. If you do this, send the dish to the table with a sprinkle of unsprayed rose petals.

Churros

Churros are a popular street food in Mexico as they are in Spain. Basically a choux paste that is deep fried, they can be sweet or savoury. If you want to try the latter, omit the sugar, add some hard cheese such as Mahon or Parmesan and dust with cayenne.

SERVES 4–6

500 ml/18 fl oz/2½ cups	milk
400 g/14 oz/2¾ cups	plain flour
4 x 15 ml spoons/4 tablespoons	caster (fine) sugar
2	eggs, well beaten
	oil for deep frying
4 x 15 ml spoons/4 tablespoons	icing (confectioners') sugar } sieved
4 x 5 ml spoons/4 teaspoons	ground cinnamon } together

1) Heat the milk. When almost boiling, tip in the flour and sugar and beat hard until the mixture forms a ball. Beat in the eggs, a little at a time.

2) Heat the oil to 190°C/370°F. Either fill a forcing bag with the mixture and squeeze 5cm/2in lengths or drop teaspoonfuls of dough into the oil.

3) As the churros rise and brown, lift out, drain on kitchen paper and dust with the sugar/cinnamon mixture. Serve.

Cilicote en Almibar

Cilicote are also known as Golden Apples but this is somewhat of a misnomer as they are actually more like plums. They have a fabulous sweet sour taste and are beautifully fragrant. If they prove impossible to find, use apricots or greengages in this light compote.

SERVES 4–6

500 g/1 lb/approx. 3–4 cups	Golden Apples (see above)
150 g/5 oz/¾ cup	caster (fine) sugar
200 ml/7 fl oz/¾ cup	water
1	vanilla pod, slit open
1	clove
a small stick	of cinnamon
a long strip	of lime peel

1) Put everything in a pan with a tight fitting lid. Bring slowly up to the boil and simmer for 10 minutes. Serve warm or well chilled.

Cook's Note
If liked, remove the warm Golden Apples and place on a glass dish. Reduce the syrup until very thick then dribble over the fruit.

Flan with Mexican Fruit Salad

Flan is very popular in Mexico. We are perhaps more familiar with it as crème caramel. Instant mixes and ready-mades are available in most supermarkets. If you have more time, make your own: it doesn't take long to prepare but requires a slow cooking which puts it outside the scope of this book.

SERVES 4–6

4 x 15 ml spoons/4 tablespoons	caster sugar
	finely grated rind and juice of a lime
125 ml/4 fl oz/½ cup	water
2	guavas, peeled and cubed
1	large avocado, peeled and cubed
1	grenadillo or 2 small passion fruits
1	small pineapple, peeled and cubed
2	pitahaya, peeled and cubed
1	large ripe mango, peeled and cubed
6	individual crème caramels
2 x 15 ml spoons/2 tablespoons	toasted flaked almonds
2 x 15 ml spoons/2 tablespoons	toasted flaked coconut

1) Dissolve the sugar in the lime juice and water. Bring to the boil. Add the guavas.
2) Simmer for 5 minutes then add the rest of the fruits, scraping in the contents of the grenadillo or passion fruit, and the lime zest. Chill.
3) To serve, unmold the crème caramels. Surround with the fruit salad and scatter over the flaked almonds and coconut.

Helado de Coco

You will need a sorbetière or ice cream maker for this quick coconut ice cream. Although you need to make sure you freeze the bowl for at least 24 hours beforehand, the actual 'working' time in this recipe is very short.

Do use the rum as the alcohol prevents the ice freezing too hard.

SERVES 4–6

400 ml/14 fl oz can	coconut milk, shaken
6 x 15 ml spoons/6 tablespoons	golden (corn) syrup ⎫ mixed
6 x 15 ml spoons/6 tablespoons	hot water ⎭ together
285 ml/½ pint/1 cup + 3 tablespoons	single cream (half and half)
2 x 15 ml spoons/2 tablespoons	rum

1) Beat everything together with a large whisk and pour into the ice cream maker as the paddles are churning. Let the machine run until the mixture is frozen – depending on type, this is 10–25 minutes.
2) Serve or scrape into a plastic box, seal and freeze for later use.

Cook's Note
This ice cream is delicious with a drizzle of grenadine or lime syrup.

Leche Quemada

This is a very sweet, rich pudding. Unless you have a very sweet tooth I suggest you use the fudgey caramel as a filling or topping. Personally, I prefer it over ice cream or on a steamed pudding or plain sponge.

Authentically, this dish takes hours to prepare – time is slashed in this recipe by using evaporated milk. The result is opaque and a little thicker. A commercially prepared milk caramel is sold in jars in supermarkets to spread on bread. This can be reheated with a little rum to make an excellent substitute. Other options for a similar milk caramel are the old boarding school treat of boiling a tin of condensed milk but this takes rather longer than 30 minutes.

Alice B. Toklas recounts the mysterious Señora B.'s recipe for *Dulce* in her cookbook and then gives her own, adding somewhat sniffily 'There are people who like it a lot.'

SERVES 4–6

400 ml/14 fl oz can	evaporated milk
200 g/7 oz/1 cup	light brown sugar
a pinch	of bicarbonate of soda (baking soda)
2 x 15 ml spoons/2 tablespoons	rum

1) Melt the sugar slowly in the milk, stirring to dissolve. When you can no longer hear grittiness, add the bicarbonate of soda (baking soda) and bring the milk to the boil. Cook, stirring, while the mixture darkens and thickens. Beat in the rum and serve.

Cook's Note
Nuts – pecans, almonds and walnuts – or coconut can be added. This caramel is also delicious over fresh sliced pears, hulled strawberries and halved peaches.

Lime & Almond Clusters

Known simply as *dulce* – sweets (candies), these are often made for Mexico's big celebration for the Day of the Dead. Looked at from afar, the preparations for the festivities seem gruesome or morbid. Children are given sugar skulls or coffins with their names piped on them. Elaborate cakes and sweetmeats are taken to the graves of dead relatives. However, in a country where many families are touched by early death, it is a way of remembering loved ones and it seems more relevant than the commercialised festivities of Halloween.

SERVES 4–6

125 ml/4 fl oz/½ cup	evaporated milk
300 g/10 oz/1½ cups	sugar
	juice and rind of a lime
75 g/2½ oz/½ cup	flaked almonds

1) Heat the milk with two thirds of the sugar.
2) In a separate pan, melt the remaining sugar. As it begins to caramelise, slowly add the juice of the lime. Add the sweetened milk. Boil to 112°C/234°F – the soft ball stage.
3) Beat in the almonds and then place spoonfuls on a greased baking sheet to cool.

Nieve

Nieve brings back simple childhood memories – *Mr Frostie*, a toy for making shaved ice will come back into his own here. Those unlucky enough never to have made his acquaintance will have to make do with a heavy duty blender.

SERVES 6
6 cups of shaved ice
6 x 15 ml spoons/6 tablespoons grenadine syrup
a few mint leaves

1) Divide the ice between 6 sundae glasses, pour over the syrup and top with the mint leaves. Easy!

Cook's Note
Other liqueurs or fruit syrups can be used. *Kahlua* (coffee), *Curaçao* (orange), concentrated apple juice or lemon or lime syrup are especially good.

Nuez con Caramelo

Mexicans have rather a sweet tooth. This version of nut brittle with pecans is found all over. Others made with peanuts, walnuts (nuez de Castilla) and seeds also exist.

SERVES 4–6

200 g/7 oz/1 cup   light brown sugar
120 g/4 oz/1 cup   shelled pecans

1) Melt the sugar slowly in a heavy based pan, stirring constantly. When it caramelises (the 'crack stage' – 154°C/310°F on a sugar thermometer), stir in the pecans.
2) Spread out onto a lightly oiled baking sheet, cool then break into pieces.

Sweet Chimichangas

SERVES 4–6

	3 large ripe bananas, halved
2 x 15 ml spoons/2 tablespoons	light muscovado sugar
2 x 5 ml spoons/2 teaspoons	ground cinnamon
	6 flour tortillas
	1 orange or lime
	oil or butter for frying
	crème fraîche

} mixed together

1) Dust the banana halves in the sugar and spice.

2) Place one half on each tortilla. Squeeze over a little juice from the orange or lime.

3) Fold up the bottom of the tortilla over the banana. Fold in the sides, roll up and secure with a cocktail stick (toothpick).

4) Fry in the oil or butter and serve immediately with some crème fraîche.

Sweet Fried Bananas

This gooey sweet mess is delicious on its own or used as a topping for store-bought or home-made ice cream. Alternatively, serve as a cheesecake topping or with an egg custard – set or pouring. Authentically, it would be served with thick soured cream – use crème fraîche as the best widely available substitute.

SERVES 4–6

75 g/2¾ oz/⅓ cup	butter
4–5	medium bananas, sliced
60 g/2 oz/½ cup	flaked almonds or pecan halves
100 g/3½ oz/½ cup	light brown muscovado sugar
2 x 5 ml spoons/2 teaspoons	ground cinnamon
2 x 15 ml spoons/2 tablespoons	rum or orange juice

1) Melt the butter and fry the bananas until lightly brown.
2) Add the nuts and fry another minute before adding the remaining ingredients. Stir carefully until the sugar has melted and the mixture is bubbling. Serve.

Cook's Note
Two squares of Mexican chocolate or good plain chocolate can be added to the bananas just before serving. Stir gently to melt into the mixture.

Sweet Tamales

If you don't have any coconut milk use dairy milk or even pineapple juice instead. In the summer months try adding wild strawberries, currants or blueberries in place of the candied fruit.

SERVES 4–6

175 g/6 oz/1 cup	instant polenta
200 ml/7 fl oz/³⁄₄ cups	coconut milk
125 ml/4½ fl oz/½ cup	water
2 x 15 ml spoons/2 tablespoons	light muscovado sugar
2 x 15 ml spoons/2 tablespoons	candied fruit – pineapple, mango, papaya – chopped
	OR
2 x 15 ml spoons/2 tablespoons	raisins

1) Mix everything in a pan and cook until it leaves the sides cleanly.
2) Shape into cigars and roll loosely in baking paper twisting the ends. Place in a steamer over boiling water for 20 minutes and serve.

Cook's Note
After steaming, the sweet tamales can be fried in butter and dusted with a mixture of ground cinnamon and icing (confectioners' sugar).

'Tuna Salad'

There's nothing fishy about this. Tuna is the Mexican Spanish name for cactus fruit or prickly pears. You may also see them sold as barbary figs. Take care when handling them as they are prickly! Small sharp hairs stick out of little knobbles on the yellowy skin, so wear gloves. If you cannot find prickly pears, the similar pitahaya can be substituted instead – they don't bite but the flavour is blander.

SERVES 4–6

6	prickly pears
½	a lime
1–2 x 15 ml spoons/ 2 tablespoons	caster (fine) sugar } mixed
5 ml spoon/1 teaspoon	ground ginger } together

1) Cut a thin slice from the top and bottom of the prickly pears, then slit the skin lengthways but not too deeply. Peel away the skin and take out the flesh. Sometimes it is a vivid pinky purple and at others an apricot yellow. Cut into chunks and place on a glass plate.
2) Squeeze over the lime and sprinkle with the sugar and ginger. Leave in a cool place until serving.

Zapote

The names of this hard leathery-skinned plum sized fruit are a bit mixed up – you might also find sapote or sapodilla. Whatever their name, wait until they are rather squishy (their names apparently derive from the Aztec 'tzapotl' meaning soft). The under-ripe fruit is white inside, when ready it turns a custardy yellow. You can use them for milkshakes too.

SERVES 4–6

500 g/1 lb/4 cups	sapodillas
	caster sugar to taste
5 ml spoon/1 teaspoon	zest of orange, lemon or lime

1) Halve the fruit, throw away the central pits and scoop out the middles and place in a serving bowl.
2) Mash with a fork, adding sugar to taste. Serve garnished with the citrus zest.

Cook's Note
You can serve these more simply – just scoop with a small teaspoon like you would an avocado.

Drinks

Agua de Jamaica

Indistinguishable from the Egyptian *Karkade*, this beautiful ruby coloured drink can be served hot or cold. The dried flowers are from the hibiscus and can be found in most wholefood shops and some supermarkets. They are even available in tea bags!

SERVES 4–6

50 g/1¾ oz/1 cup	hibiscus flowers
1 litre/1¾ pints/4 cups	water
	sugar to taste
	cinammon sticks, 1 per glass

1) Bring the hibiscus flowers and water to the boil.
2) Leave in a warm place to steep for 20 minutes.
3) Strain through a paper coffee filter and sweeten to taste.
4) Serve with a cinnamon stick in each glass. To serve cold, chill well.

Café de Olla

Coffee in the Middle East is very similar to this Mexican version: simply exchange cardamom for the cinnamon. This is an intensely flavoured, very warming brew, ideal for those of us who live in chillier climes.

SERVES 4–6

500 ml/18 fl oz/2 cups	water
2	cinnamon sticks
1–2	cloves
4 x 15 ml spoons/4 tablespoons	freshly ground coffee – use a superfine grind
3–6 x 15 ml spoons/ 3–6 tablespoons	brown sugar (to taste – with 6 it is almost syrupy)

1) Combine everything in a coffee pot or saucepan. Heat until just simmering, stirring occasionally. Keep warm. Strain and serve.

Horchata

Horchata in Mexico varies enormously. Sometimes it is made with rice, sometimes with melon seeds or almonds. If you think this a little odd, remember that Lemon Barley water is the British equivalent. The main ingredient in this horchata is tiger nuts – the original Spanish ingredient. These are not really nuts at all but rather shrivelled-looking tubers. They are also known as *chufas* in Spain or 'earth almonds'. A bag of tiger nuts will keep you quiet for hours as they are quite chewy and are like munching fresh coconut, even though your jaws ache, you can't quite stop!

This is an all together more civilised way of consuming them, especially if you add a shot of *Kahlua* (Mexican coffee liqueur) to the horchata first.

SERVES 4–6

150 g/5 oz/1 cup tiger nuts
625 ml/1¼ pints/2½ cups cold water
sugar to taste (optional)

1) Grind the nuts in a heavy duty blender, liquidizer or food processor with a little of the water. Add the remaining water and whizz briefly.
2) Strain into a jug and serve cold, adding sugar to taste if desired.

Cook's Note
It is not unusual for lime to be added to the horchata or, as described above, *Kahlua* can be added or a little cinnamon.

Hot Chocolate

Banish winter blues with a steaming mug of this – it beats any commercially available powdered drink and really doesn't take much longer to make. If you can find Mexican chocolate, you can omit the almond and cinnamon. Use milk or water or half and half.

SERVES 4–6

750 ml/1¼ pints/3 cups	milk (or see above)
2 x 15 ml spoons/2 tablespoons	ground almonds
1 stick	cinnamon
100 g/3½ oz/½ cup	plain chocolate, grated
5 ml spoon/1 teaspoon	ground cinnamon

1) Heat the milk with the almond and cinnamon. Keep hot for 5 minutes, allowing the flavours to infuse.
2) Strain onto the chocolate in a warm jug and whisk until the chocolate has melted into the milk.
3) Pour into individual mugs and serve with a sprinkle of cinnamon.

Licuado de Agua

Instead of a milky fruit shake, this one's made with water and fruit. It can also be made with sparkling water. Instead of using sugar, you could try adding a fruit syrup, such as grenadine, to add colour, flavour and sweetness. Substitute whichever fruit you have to hand – peaches, nectarines and papaya all make great drinks.

SERVES 4–6

1	medium pineapple, peeled, cored and cut into chunks
1 litre/1¾ pints/4 cups	ice cold water
	sugar to taste – depends on the sweetness of the fruit
	mint sprigs
	lime slices

1) Whizz the pineapple and water in a blender.
2) Strain into a jug and sweeten. Float the mint and lime on the top.

Sangritas

Tomato juice never tasted like this before. Use this non-alcoholic drink as a starter or aperitif. You can, if liked, add Tequila to taste.

	SERVES 4
	juice of 3 limes
	salt
1–2	small red Pequin or Birdseye chillies, crushed and chopped
300 ml/12 fl oz	tomato juice
150 ml/5 fl oz	freshly squeezed orange juice
2–3 x 15 ml spoons/ 2–3 tablespoons	grenadine syrup

1) Dip or brush the rims of 4 glasses in or with the lime juice then dip in the salt. Chill well.
2) Combine the remaining lime juice with a pinch of salt.
3) Add the rest of the ingredients.
4) Leave in a cold place until serving then strain into the prepared glasses.

Margarita

There seem to be as many ways to make a Margarita, that archetypal Mexican cocktail, as there are to make the perfect Martini. Here is just one.

SERVES 6

250 ml/9 fl oz/1 cup	tequila
125 ml/4 fl oz/½ cup	Cointreau or other orange liqueur
125 ml/4 fl oz/½ cup	lime juice
	ice
	fresh strawberries or peaches, sliced
6	sprigs of mint

1) Mix the liquids together.
2) Divide the ice between 6 chilled glasses. (See the Sangritas recipe on page 142 for how to frost the rims.)
3) Add fruit to the glasses and pour over the tequila mixture. Top each with a sprig of mint.

Mexican Chocolate II

This is a grown up sophisticated version of hot chocolate. It is very rich and smooth – it can be served instead of or after dessert.

SERVES 4–6

50 g/2 oz/⅓ cup	chocolate, grated
5 ml spoon/1 teaspoon	ground cinnamon
2–4 x 15 ml spoons/	
2–4 tablespoons	sugar
125 ml/4½ fl oz/½ cup	boiling water
125 ml/4½ fl oz/½ cup	hot milk
125 ml/4½ fl oz/½ cup	hot strong coffee
	a little orange rind
15 ml spoon/1 tablespoon	sherry

1) In a bowl over barely simmering water, melt the chocolate with the cinnamon and sugar. When melted, whisk in the boiling water. Stir frequently for 2 minutes, then whisk in the milk, coffee, orange rind and sherry. Pour into small cups and serve.

Mexican Strawberry Milkshakes

One that kids of every age will really enjoy – in Spanish it is *licuado de leche*.

SERVES 6

1 litre/1¾ pints/4 cups	cold milk
450 g/1 lb/3¼ cups	small ripe strawberries, hulled
4 x 15 ml spoons/4 tablespoons	caster (fine) sugar – add more to taste
6	sprig of mint

1) Whizz all of the ingredients in the blender until smooth. Strain and serve with a sprig of mint on each tall glass.

Té

Tea in Mexico normally means a herb tea. The two most common are *Manzanillo* (chamomile) or *Yerbabuena* (mint). The method is the same in both cases. The teas are usually served at the end of the meal as a digestif, much like Pedro Conejo (Peter Rabbit) was dosed after overeating in Mr MacGregor's vegetable patch!

SERVES 4–6
25 g/1 oz dried chamomile flowers or mint leaves
500 ml/1 pint/2 cups boiling water
sugar to taste

1) Put the chamomile or mint into a clean teapot. Pour on the boiling water and leave to infuse for 5 minutes. Strain into cups and sweeten to taste.

Cook's Note
Herbal teas are available in bags – however, check for additives, many now come with extra flavourings. A straightforward tea is required for authenticity.

Index